Pigspurt
– or Six Pigs from Happiness

KEN CAMPBELL founded the Science Fiction Theatre of Liverpool in 1976 where he directed two monumental epics: the twenty-two hour cult show *The Warp* and *Illuminatus!*, which was chosen to open the Cottesloe at the National Theatre in London. He also founded the legendary *Ken Campbell's Roadshow*. He is the author of such children's plays as *Old King Cole*, *Skungpoomery*, *School for Clowns*, *Clowns on a School Outing*, *Peef* and *Frank 'n' Stein*, plus books for two musicals: *Bendigo* and *Walking Like Geoffrey*. His film scripts have included *Unfair Exchanges*, which starred Julie Walters and *The Madness Museum*, in which Ken Campbell played the Proprietor of the asylum. His previous semi-autobiographical show, *Furtive Nudist*, was published in 1992. He is well known to television audiences for his portrayal of Fred Johnson, Alf Garnett's neighbour in *In Sickness and in Health*.

'Three cheers for Ken Campbell's *Pigspurt* in which the erstwhile furtive nudist free-associates his way through nursery school and rep memories, an obsession with noses, Ken Dodd, faith healing and other random mental debris which finally coalesces in a burst of pink light and a sense that the riddle of the universe has been solved. There is nobody else like him.'

Irving Wardle, *The Independent on Sunday*

'A full stop could well be a hyphen coming straight at you —'

Ken Campbell

Ken Campbell

PIGSPURT

— *or Six Pigs from Happiness*

Drawings by Eve Stewart

Methuen Drama

First published in Great Britain 1993
by Methuen Drama
an imprint of Reed Consumer Books Ltd
Michelin House, 81 Fulham Road, London SW3 9RB
and Auckland, Melbourne, Singapore and Toronto
and distributed in the United States of America by
Heinemann, a division of Reed Publishing (USA) Inc.,
361 Hanover Street, Portsmouth, New Hampshire NH 03801 3959

A CIP catalogue record for this book
is available at the British Library
ISBN 0 413 68100 9

Typeset by Falcon Graphic Art Ltd
Wallington, Surrey
Printed in Great Britain by Clays Ltd, St Ives plc

Caution

'Like Stanislavsky and Brecht, I've invented an entirely new method of acting, I call it the *enantiodromic approach*. The theory of enantiodromia is that the left and right sides of your face represent different personalities. If you're clever with mirrors you'll see what I mean. My right side, for instance, is that of an inept housewife and the left side – or 'facet' as we call it – is that of a spanking squire!'

Ken Campbell

Pigspurt
– or Six Pigs from Happiness

Pigspurt
– or Six Pigs From Happiness

Written and performed by Ken Campbell, *Pigspurt* was
premièred at the Riverside Studios, London and transferred to
the Almeida Theatre, London in 1992 before embarking on a
tour of the UK, Amsterdam and, in 1993, Australia and the
Royal National Theatre, London.

Pigspurt theme and incidental music by Richard Kilgour

'**** Nose' by Buster Bloodvessel (Bad Manners)

Paintings and props by Mitch Davies

Produced by Colin Watkeys

'He's all right. He's all right' —
People are always coming up to me and saying 'How's Alf?'
  because they recognize me from the *In Sickness and in Health*
  thing —
They don't know my name, they don't know my character's
  name and so they say:
'How's Alf?' —
And I say: 'He's all right' —
Sometimes they pop up from holes in the road: 'How's Alf?'
  'He's all right' —
They break ranks from National Front marches: 'How's Alf?'
  Fuck off. 'He's all right.'

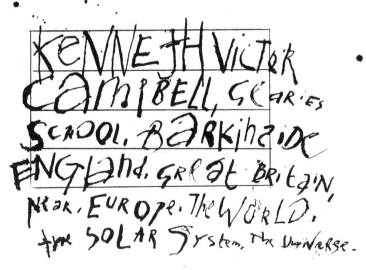

That's the style of thing we used to write on our exercise
   books when we were six and three-quarters —
in case the things got lost in space.

My first brush with show business was at Gearies School —
Showtime on Friday afternoons —
Being born in the war we didn't have many toys —
And so the form was if you'd got a toy no one had seen yet,
   you'd bring it along on a Friday afternoon and show it to the
   other kids.

But one afternoon our Showtime was cancelled —
And our class (we were Miss O'Halloran's class) —
were put together with Mrs Denn's class —
And the subject was GOD.

Apparently we are all born with a bit of the Almighty inside us —
we've all got our bit of God —
and it's situated somewhere in the stomach region —
And every time you do something a little bit naughty —
like tell a lie —
(apparently writing a lie is even worse) —
you get a little bit of *dirty in your God*.

Did you know that recently there'd been chaps applying for
    entry Up There —
and their Gods *had been filthy*? —
There'd been cases of fellows whose Gods had been completely
    eaten away —
'Yes, Janet?' (A question from Janet Dean at the back) —
'Do you mean Germans, Miss O'Halloran?' —
'Yes, Janet, very good' —
Lately, people who'd been applying for entrance Up There
    with totally eaten away Gods had been Germans —
And a few Japanese —
Listen! Mrs Denn is going to be most upset *indeed* if any of
    our year are caught applying for entrance Up There with
    completely eaten away Gods.

And now, to help us with the concept —
we're only six and three-quarters —
some of us are only six-and-a-half! —
are handed round autopsy liver photographs —
First the photo of the liver of a terminal alcoholic —
which we have to compare with the fine frisky liver of a healthy-
    living sort of chap —
(Really a quite striking afternoon) —
'Yes? Yes, Janet?' —
Janet wants to know, is there any way you can clean up your
    God —
'Yes Janet, we're glad you asked that, of course there is —
of course there's a way you can clean up your God' —
What you've got to do: you've got to do two good things
    for every one bad thing —
Two to one is the ratio.

Also slippering —
Slippering will help —
Having the backs of your legs (Miss O'Halloran) or your bottom
    (Mrs Denn) bashed at with a shoe —
that'll get it down a bit —
But you're still going to have to do one good thing —
'Yes Peter?' —
A question from Peter Sarbutt —
Peter wants to know, can you meet God without dying —
'Yes, Peter, you can. But it will be *in the most unlikely place*' —
This gives rise to a lot of conjecture in the playground —
as to where that might be —
we can think up some very unlikely places! —
But no!! —
If you can *think* of it, it won't be it!!! —
It'll be *even more unlikely than that*!!!!

Every morning you've got to write up your diary —
Even if nothing's happened to you —
you've still got to write about it —
you've got to put it in your diary —
But if anything a wee bit sensational has happened to you —
maybe you'll have the honour of reading out your diary to
    Miss O'Halloran and the class —
And I used to like to go for that honour —
But very often this would mean *lying in my diary*.

So a dubious glory —
but as I go back to my desk —
I can feel the dirtiness gnawing into my God.

But I manage to get hold of Him —
got Him on the direct line —
'It's alright actually sir, all this lying I've been doing in my
diary because I won't ever be doing that again, lying in my
   diary, and anyway I'll be doing two good things for it, and
   two good things for yesterday's one as well . . .' —
Maybe I ought to make a full confession of everything —
request a programme of slippering from Mrs Denn and Miss
   O'Halloran —
Get the odds in my favour —
(Mind, it didn't sound too great Up There —
all that hymn singing —
But I'd enjoy the flying —
and definitely to be preferred to the alternative as outlined
   by Mrs Denn.)

I wrote a little poem at this time which went:

   'My diary is a liary
   A diary of lies
   My God-all-dirty diary
   In heaven for me no pies' —

And even to this day, if I repeat over and over again:
'No pies . . . *No pies* . . . There's going to be NO PIES for
   you, Kenneth!'
Tears stream down my face.

About six months after Dirtying-up-your-God-Friday a new boy
    was put into the school and he was put into the desk next to
    mine —
and we became best friends —
His name was Derek —
and one playtime I unburdened myself on Derek as to all
    this lying I'd been doing in my diary —
But Derek said:
(but Derek had not had the benefit of autopsy liver photographs)
'Not to worry, because there's *no such thing as God* —
and anyway He's stupid.' —
Sometimes I felt that Derek had maybe three-quarters convinced
    me —
Sometimes I could be almost as happy and breezy as Derek.

Sad to relate, when Derek was eleven, his mother (a devout
  Methodist) chopped him to bits —
Some of the bits weren't found —
And the *Ilford Recorder* which covered all the sensational aspects
  of the case in every detail, didn't tell us —
maybe they didn't know —
whether or not this was down to a *theological altercation*.

'For you Carstairs, it is the —' —
I am attempting an impression of the late Stuart Pearce —
When I left the Royal Academy of Dramatic Art in 1960, after
    a lot of letters they eventually let me in at the Colchester
    Repertattery Company —
a weekly Rep establishment —
and undoubtedly the God there was Stuart Pearce.
Stuart Pearce was probably the last in that great line of 'actor-
    laddies' —
This means that, equipped with a silver-topped cane, you greet
    younger members of the Co, like myself, with *'Hello, dear
    boy!'* —
Stuart had toured in the war years with the Tod Slaughter
    Melodrama Company —
and he styled himself *'eccentric character actor'* —
And this means that you deliver your many and varied
    performances *through your nose* —
For Stuart Pearce it was like his piercer was his nose —
an extraordinary prying, enquiring, prodding, poking organ —
Indeed it was Stuart's pride that by the Friday —
(these shows only lasted a week) —
that by the Friday, Stuart would have contrived to be touching
    his nose upon the nose of a fellow actor —
(Dramatically justified, in a sense, by Stuart's baroque, heavily
    ornamented performance style —)
Which of course led to a lot of tension if you were on stage
    with Stuart in the early part of the week —
when the nose was seeking out its Friday quarry.

Sensational he was on the Friday of some
    thriller —
Goes Stuart: '*A knife in the back . . . is not what we call*
    . . . a normal death, CARSTAIRS!' —
Stuart's piercer-nose narrowly missing the Carstairs hooter but
    catching him on the cheek —
and cutting it! —
He'd sliced Carstairs' cheek with his nose! —
continuing: – '*For you Carstairs, it is the* —' —
and he spells it out with his now crimson-tipped nose:

'e ... a ... d ...' –

How had Stuart done it? —
How had he cut Carstairs with his nose? —
Various theories . . .
some said that Stuart must have glued up his nose a shard
    of razor blade —
others said he had simply crushed a blood capsule in his nostril
    and snotted it at Carstairs.

When Stuart left Colchester to go off to finer things with
the Penguin Players, the place was a bit desolate —
But then, at Christmas: the panto —
and we had Hugh Hastings playing the piano —
And Hugh Hastings was a name in those days —
Hugh Hastings had written a naval comedy —
It had been on in the West End: *Seagulls Over Sorrento* —
But by this time nobody much was doing it —
it was just being done in prisons —
and Hugh Hastings was reduced to playing the piano for the
    Colchester Repertattery panto —

Anyway, I was having a drink with Hugh in the pub one
    lunchtime and Hugh started talking about his acting career —
Well actually I hadn't known he'd got one —
A multi-talent: writing naval comedies, playing the piano . . .
    and now an acting career —
But this was the extraordinary thing: Hugh Hastings was only
    interested in playing Third Act Detective Inspectors in
    thrillers —
THIRD ACT DETECTIVE INSPECTORS!? —
they're the sort of part you get lumbered with, aren't they? —
hardly, surely, a career goal? —
'Oh no no no!' —
Not according to Hugh —
'No!' he said. 'No' —
He said: 'The Third Act Detective Inspector is the nearest
    thing we have today to the fine old tradition of *deus ex*
    machina!' —
What's that!? —
Well, in order to understand *deus ex machina* you've got to
    go back in time —
Evidently the ancient Greeks, Sophocles and Co, if they'd've
    got their plots to such a pass that they couldn't logically
    resolve them —
it would be time then to call down the *deus ex machina* —
The *deus* being the god, and the *machina* this bunch of cogs
    and rope and wotnot —
And the god comes clanking down —
and with his deific powers he'd be able to put things in harmony
    again —
And Hugh said: 'Isn't that the same as your Third Act Detective
    Inspector? —
You've got two-and-a-half acts of human beings fucking up,
    and then, Whoomph! —
The Inspector calls! —
And with his metropolitan magic he puts things back in order?
'No, no,' said Hugh, 'a Third Act Detective Inspector —

Man, it's a *theophany*.* —
With a Third Act Detective Inspector you can romp away
   with the thunder with the GLORY of any thriller —
if you know the secret' —
'Well,' I said. 'Here's another half, Hugh —
A secret? You mean there's a secret to playing Third Act
   Detective Inspectors?' —
'Mmm,' he said, 'oh yes —
first of all, you've got to learn the lines' —
And that was revolutionary talk in those days —
Learn the lines? —
you always played a Third Act Detective Inspector with a
   notebook —
you'd got all your lines written in the notebook —
(poised as if to write answer – in fact reading line: —
'And where were you on the night of the fourteenth?') —
Hugh said, 'Don't even *have* a notebook —
And then,' he said (and this is the big one) —
'look for clues.' —
Wow —
'Where were you . . . (looking under hat) —
on the night of er . . . (finding sausage) —
the fourteenth? . . .' (examining sausage with magnifying glass) —
Wow —

And now life is minutes on a clock until I get a Third Act
   Detective Inspector —
and sooner or later, I thought, I gotta get one —
and it was later —
The drama to be *Signpost to Murder* by Monte Doyle —

Theophany: n., pl. -ies. A manifestation of a deity to a man in a form that, though visible,
is not necessarily material. [*Chambers Dictionary*]

me to play Inspector Bickford, coming on (classically) halfway
    through Act Three —
We had a new leading man that week, a fellow called Ted
    Webster —
the lead part being a lunatic —
a very dangerous lunatic escaped from the lunatic asylum —
He bursts in on a lone woman in a country house —
he begins to molest, to maraud her —
Then, towards the end of Act Two —
it begins to transpire that —
just possibly —
she's ghastlier, she's pottier than he is! Ha Ha! —
But then . . . —
Well, I'm not going to spoil it for you —
If David Hare's suddenly running out of steam
they may be wanting to mount a Monte Doyle revival season.

Anyway, for a Third Act Detective Inspector at Colchester
    in 1960, you only had two mornings' rehearsal —
The first rehearsal: director Bernard Kelly looks up over his
    half-glasses and says, 'You're not using a notebook, Ken?' —
I said, 'No Bernard, I thought I'd learn the lines.' —
'Learn the lines!' —
company exchanging 'Whoops ducky!' looks —
Since merely learning the lines so phased everyone, I thought
    I'd better not look for clues at the rehearsal —
I didn't want to get that cut —
But I was looking around for the sort of places you might
    look for clues come the opening night —
Indeed I had a scheme developing to secrete sundry clues
    in and under things, both meaningful and red-herring.

Opening night Monday, and the first two-and-a-half acts had
   gone what Ted Webster and Margaret Thing, the leading
   lady, would have called 'well' —
By 'well' they'd've meant that there'd not been a chuckle —
not a titter from the house —
Therefore the good people of Colchester must have been utterly
   captivated by Monte Doyle's desperate plotting —
Then: Enter Inspector Bickford —
And I start looking for clues —
And wow! —
The whole place went up! —
A gale of laughter – Force 10! —
And the Bishop of Colchester in the front row, and he's going,
   'UH HAHH! HA-HAHHH!! UH HA!!! HA-HAHHH!!!!' —
I thought, I must remember to write a thank-you letter to
   Hugh, tell him how well it's gone —
And then at the bowing, thunderous applause —
And I thought, probably two-thirds of it is down to me —
But a few minutes later —
the metal door of my changing-hutch is burst rudely open —
And there was Ted Webster —
he'd put on a kilt for this occasion —
and he took the fire bucket off the wall —
full of old greasy water been there thirty years —
and he slung it over me and my clothes —
And you had to pay for your own clothes for shows in those
   days —
And he slung the bucket at my head, and he said:
'IT'S YOUR LIFE IF YOU TRY THAT TOMORROW!' —
Thank you for the note Ted.

Tuesday night, I didn't look for clues . . .
but for some reason . . .
this was funnier – not doing anything —
They were out of control —
And I go up to Ted and say, 'Excuse me sir, but is this
    your cigarette lighter?'
And Ted —
the pupils of his eyes juddering like a washing-machine on
    final spin —
waits till he can be heard, then says:
'YES, IT IS – **YOU FUNNY LITTLE MAN**!' —
A bit of variation on the script, that was —
And so I arrested him . . . at a distance —
Luckily Margaret Thing had to bow between me and Ted —
and at the last bow, I sailed off the stage —
and beat the audience out of the auditorium doors —
and into the little pub up the road and round the corner,
    that the company never used —
But there to be found eventually by the director Bernard Kelly —
Bernard said, 'For Christ's sake, don't come in tomorrow —
Just come in a few minutes before your entrance and then
    GET OUT FAST before the bowing, or Ted Webster will
    kill you —
And oh shit!' said Bernard, 'The Bishop's coming again
    tomorrow' —
The Bishop coming a second time to a thriller? —
The Bishop used to come to the first night of everything —
and if it was a comedy, if it was a farce, yes – he'd be
    there every night —
except for Friday when he ran the jazz club —
(What he'd do you see, on the first night he could sort out where
    all the laughs were, so that on the next nights, when he'd always

bring a couple of cubs with him, you'd see them in the front row
and the Bishop'd go: 'UH HAHH! HA-HAHHH!! UH HA!!!
HA! HAHHH!!!! boys' – and on the last 'HAHHH!!!!' he'd
grab and squeeze their knees, cubs jumping and yelping —
He was training the younger members of the scout movement
in comedy timing.) —
I said, 'Bernard, is there some way of shutting an audience
up?' —
Bernard said, 'There's only one sure-fire technique for that —
What you'd have to do,' he said, 'is as soon as you come
on, forget your lines —
Just stand there and wait until the prompter's voice has rung
round the hall and then get on with it —
You won't get a murmur out of them then.'

So the next night, in the interests of survival, that's what I
did —
I simply came on and dried —
And they were as good as gold —
To be sure, it was a bit sad seeing the pale white knees
of the cubs in the front row —
ungrasped by Holy hand —
But that's what I did for the rest of the week's run —
I just came on and dried and we heard from the prompter
and everything was fine —
And Margaret Whatever-her-name-was came up to me after
the last show
and she said, 'I just want to congratulate you on your performance
Kenneth —
We were all so worried about it at the beginning of the week —
and then from somewhere —
you found such strength' —
'Thank you,' I said, humbly, thinking: arsehole.

A footnote on the Bishop of Colchester:
It seems that in his concluding couple of years on Earth he
    wasn't changing his underpants —
He'd originally put a pair on, but then he'd left them on
    until they'd disintegrated before donning the next pair —
We deduce this because, when he died, round the body was
    found eight elasticated bands —
And I had this picture, of the Bishop Up There —
with his left hand pulling his elastics up from his tubby body
    and plucking them with his right —

b'doom   b'doom   b'doom   b'doom

(He was a musical man, ran the jazz club.)

20

Captain Charlie Charrington
It was thus I first encountered the Captain:
When I was at the Royal Academy of Dramatic Art . . . there
    was a lady student there —
and I had designs on her doughnut —
She was the daughter of a handsome Indian doctor lady
    and some British chap —
and she had this heavy black hair which she chose to do
    up on the top of her head into a doughnut —
And when the classes got tedious, I'd find my attention wandering
    over to Dee Charrington and her doughnut of hair —
And you couldn't stop them: Playful imaginings . . .
Whackiest of which possibly was the Viciously Sharpened Shears
    Scenario —
the notion of stalking Dee Charrington through the dark-lit
    corridors of RADA with my shears —
coming up behind her and Zjip! Bong! Weee! —
I never mentioned this to her, of course —
nor to anyone come to that —
But I suppose she must have seen me looking at her in a
    rather interested fashion —
and this sparked up a bit of a friendship —
And so it was me she asked if I'd like to go with her to
    meet her father —
And this was odder than it sounds, because she'd never met
    her father —
Possibly she'd been viewed by him a couple of times as a
    toddler —
She wasn't sure —
Anyway, the fellow was to be appearing in the pub round
    the corner, the Marlborough, that lunchtime.

I had always regarded the bowler hat as the pinnacle of berkery —
But not as it sat on the head of Captain Charlie Charrington! —
To be sure, I think his bowler hat was curly of brim —
snapped down at the back —
But this was 1959 —
it was to be a good few years before Steed of *The Avengers*
    had one of those jobs —
And the Captain, he exuded a dash, a panache —
His daughter Dee was a wee bit nervous —
now powdering her nose for the second time —
And I was 19 and I said to the Captain, 'What do you do
    now then sir?' —
And Captain Charlie Charrington, of the twinkling eye, took
    my hand and put it inside his jacket —
And I felt his gun —
And I think it was the Captain's gun which fired my passion —
I began to woo the Captain's daughter in earnest now —
What I mean is, in her entirety —
It wasn't just her doughnut ring we were after now.

Sad to relate, she chose to marry another and go off to Canada
    with him, taking her mother and her brother with her.
Eight years later I was writing comedy sketches for the radio —
Monday Night at Home was the programme —
And I saw that the Ideal Home Exhibition was on and I said:
'Give us a ticket and I'll try and write something funny about
    that' —
Once into Olympia, I was halted by this particular stall —
Not that there was anything particular about the stall —

it was the salesman, the pitcher —
He was *mesmeric* —
All he was selling was saws —
But not saws of the usual variety —
These saws were sort of like string —
The notion being that you'd throw one end of your saw over
    an over-hanging bough, say, and Zzzzzzzzzzzzzmmm! —
You'd saw it off —
But that wasn't the only use for these things, no —
Apparently the Gurkhas could take off a man's head in one
    with them —
they practised on goats —
And he was unloading these things like there was no tomorrow —
And you couldn't think that everyone had an over-hanging
    bough problem —
or were goat breeders with antisocial fantasies —
And there was an Indian gentleman there —
and he didn't know whether he wanted one or not —
And my new hero addresses him in an extremely foreign tongue:
'Yalla walah yillah walla yallah!' —
The fellow looked blank, so he tried him with another one:
'Rawah bawah hawah bah!' —
The fellow's still blank, but on the third one he gets him:
'Raggad ahab dallah halaba daha!' —
And the fellow went: 'Oyulla whahalla badah lilla badah ha?' —
'Oyuggah darrapah dag gadda oyehhh!' replies my man with
    mime of such drama it draws a gasp from the crowd and
    makes it difficult to walk —
and Indian fellow goes off with eight —
And then he saw me, the seller of saws saw me —
And he turned to his assistant and he said:
'We're closing for ten minutes' —
'You,' he said, 'are coming with me.'

And I followed him, I followed him out through a door which
    said NO EXIT —
and then up a darkened corridor to two mighty doors which
    said: NO ADMITTANCE —
and in we went —
And then we were in the exhibitors' canteen —
and he was getting a pot of tea for two, and a couple of
    chocolate éclairs —
and as we sat down he said:
'How's Dee?' —
The Captain! —
It was Captain Charlie Charrington, selling saws! —
'Oh! Well sir,' I said. 'I don't know —
She got married about seven or eight years ago —
went to Canada with this bloke' —
Yes yes yes! —
He had vaguely heard about this —
The Captain, he'd not seen her since that lunchtime in the pub —
Anyway, I was able to fill out the Captain's ten minutes with
    some images of his splendid daughter —
But given the fact that we'd mentioned her marriage, I was
    surprised by his last remark:
'Look after my Dee won't you,' he said —
'Yes sir,' I said, 'I will.'

And all of a sudden it was 1972 —
And it was that morning when I was supposed to be going
    to Munich —
(Why, you ask, would he be wanting to go to Munich?) —
Well, in those days I had my own travelling comedy outfit —
Ken Campbell's Roadshow —
And we were into international comedy now —
panging 40′ of elastic into Sylveste McCoy's face, snipping off

the customers' ties: the comedy of driving nails up your nose,
  and putting live ferrets down your trousers —
International comedy —
And we were about to open a three-week residency in Munich's
  legendary Fuck-The-Hell Bar —
Actually I was just the director on that one —
but I had to be there because the ferret was on a one-way ticket —
due to the rabies laws —
I hoped I'd find some friendly Kraut who'd look after the
  little fellow when the show was over —
And also, I was getting the company to try a new routine
  in Munich —
I say it was a new routine —
as a matter of fact I'd pinched it from Abbot and Costello —
It's their baseball routine: *Who's On First Base*, they call it —
But I'd done a little work on it and put it into football terms —
It's a way of muddling the opposition by giving your team
  code names —
So our version went:
  'Who's on the left-wing,
  What's on the right-wing,
  I Don't Know is centre-forward' —
  Thick Person: 'Who's on the left-wing?' —
  Answer: 'Yes!'
Seven pages of this drivel, but you can get them hysterical
  with it —
Even Germans you can get hysterical with it.

(There were a couple of Israelis came to the Fuck-The-Hell
  Bar —
So impressed were they with this that they had the thing translated
  into Hebrew —

And they had me flown over to Tel Aviv to direct the
operations —
And I'll give you my Hebrew now:
'Mi bagaff hasmali,
Ma bagaff himani,
Ani lo yudiah haloutz ma kazi.
That's:
'Who's on the left-wing,
What's on the right-wing,
I Don't Know is centre-forward.'
And I've got another bit of Hebrew —
Before *'Mi bagaff hasmali, Ma bagaff himani, Ani lo yudiah*
haloutz ma kazi' got drummed into the director's head, I
worked up another one —
because in those days in Tel Aviv there seemed to be a lot
of Hebrew speakers who didn't know where they were —
They'd come up to me with their maps and their charts and
ask directions in a very demanding way —
I don't know why they thought I'd know the way —
but I thought it would be sporting if I could get rid of them
in Hebrew —
And I was in a café on the Dizengoff and the proprietor had
thoughtfully put in the menu helpful Hebrew phrases for the
visitor in phonetic English —
And I put together a slightly surreal reply for these occasions:
'Ani rotzah lekuleff tapuzeem.'
Which translates as: 'Excuse me, I wish to peel oranges.'
So when I got asked directions now, I'd say:
'Ani rotzah lekuleff tapuzeem!' —
Sometimes I think they'd hear my English accent coming through
and reply: 'Really? What – right away old boy?'
'Ani rotzah lekuleff tapuzeem!' —
'But you're not a woman!'
'What? No no. That's true, I'm not a woman, no . . . but this
is a country, young as it is, where a man may peel an orange,
isn't it?' —

'No no no,' he said. ' "*Ani rotzah*" is the feminine form; what you're saying there is "I, *a lady*, wish to peel oranges." ')

Anyway, I'd missed the first train-boat-train to Munich due to some farce in Dave Hill's kitchen the night before —

And I seemed to be doing nothing about catching the second one —

And it wasn't like it was going to be dull company in Munich —

Marcel Steiner had just invented his smallest theatre in the world —

his two-seater theatre he'd built on the side-car of his motor-bike —

And Alan Devlin was going to be there doing his comedy drunk heckling if he wasn't too pissed —

And then I realized I was paralysed —

I assumed it was terminal —

And the phrase that came to mind was: Entropy of the bone marrow —

That's what I'd got —

And that's why I missed the midnight train —

I can remember looking at myself in the mirror, and saying:

'You're all hollowed out Kenif —

It's all gone a-crumble' —

And the only thing working was the elbows —

And so I levered myself up by the elbows —

and I elbowed myself to bed, falling eventually into a stiff sleep —

to be awoken about 3 o'clock in the morning by the telephone ringing —

And it was Dee Charrington phoning me from Toronto —

And she wanted to be talking about her father —

'Your father Dee?' I said. 'You mean the Captain.' —

And just saying those words: 'The Captain!' —

It flushed all the entropy out of the bone marrow —

and I was ready for anything —
Dee informed me that her father the Captain had died —
He'd died in mysterious circumstances in Oman —
and the body had now been flown back to England —
And neither she nor her mother could attend the funeral (which
    was to be on the Thursday) and could I stand in for them? —
I said, 'Well yes. Yes, I'd be pleased to do that for you, Dee.' —
In that event, would I ring this telephone number —
the number of a certain Doris Kontardi —
Doris Kontardi had accompanied the Captain's body back to
    England —
I said, 'Well, it's about half-past three in the morning now Dee —
Shall I leave it till later?' —
She'd got a Canadian voice now —
She said, *'I'd rather you rang now.'*

So there we are, the Captain dead —
Died in mysterious circumstances in Oman —
And now, phoning up Doris Kontardi —
And speaking to a veddy posh voice —
Veddy posh people put dees where their arrs should be —
So not 'very' but 'veddy' —
And not 'Doris' but 'Doddis': Doddis Kontardi —
And she, Doddis Kontardi, was an archaeologist lady, and
    she'd been commissioned by the Sultan of Oman to dig up
    stuff round Muskat to stock a little museum there for the
    tourists —
And her archaeological site facilitator —
known (wonderfully) locally as Sheik Fixit —
had been Captain Charlie Charrington —
Evidently ideal for the position since he knew every nuance
    of Arabic from Morroco to the Gulf —
'But,' said Doddis, 'there'd been film people there —

and there'd been something of a party —
and everybody had wanted the Captain to stay —
But he'd met an old friend, and he'd said —
'No, there is something I must do.' —
And he'd gone off into the desert with the old friend —
And we don't think it was the heart attack which was fatal —
It was the fall backwards on the rocks . . .' —
But there was doubt in Doddis Kontardi's voice as to whether
    that is what had really happened —
She said, 'Will Dee be coming to the funeral, and her mother?' —
I said, 'No no, I'm afraid they can't make it, —
they've asked me to stand in for them.'
But then, with inspiration, I said:
'But maybe her brother will come – maybe Paul will come' —
She said: *'The Captain had a son??!'* —
'Well,' I said, 'I'm not *totally* sure about that —
Maybe he didn't —
I don't know —
But if he did, his name might be Paul —
I think —
But as I say, I'm not sure' —

Then back to Dee —
I said, 'That Kontardi's very worried about the *existence* of
    your brother Paul' —
She said,'Paul will be there —
Can he stay with you?' —
Yeah, sure —
And Paul arrived and I said:
'How well did you know your father Paul?' —
He said, 'I met him on four occasions —
Once when I was five, once when I was eleven, once when
    I was fifteen, and once when I was nineteen' —

I said: 'When did you first feel the gun?' —
He said: 'I first felt the gun when I was five —
I felt the gun again when I was eleven —
And when I was eleven I was also shown the uncut gems, and
    pointed to the X marking the spot on a certain Island in the
    South Pacific —
Also I was instructed this way:
that if our paths were ever to chance to meet, I must never
    call the man "Dad" or "Father" —
the name was always to be Charlie, or —
The Captain.'

Crossword enthusiasts will know this, that the favourite anagram
    in the *Guardian* for 'funeral' is 'real fun' —
And so it was with the Captain's —
A proper burial for the Captain —
and four weeping women round the grave:
Doddis; a chummy lady name of Sammy; and a Venus in
    Furs (Gwendoline) —
And the Captain had been living with the three of them at
    the same time —
but unbeknown to each other —
And they all met round the grave —
And the Venus in Furs had brought along several male shoulders
    to swoon and to weep on —
but not Sammy, and not Doddis —
And so Paul and I took them off to the pub for a nostalge
    about the Captain —
leaving behind the fourth lady —
We never got to know who she was —
the lone and anonymous griever at the graveside —
In the Pub, Doddis silent with her gin —
one supposes hurt by the rude discovery of the Captain's two,

possibly three, other ladies —
But Sammy recalling for us the first time she met the Captain —
In Aden . . . a military airfield —
and to her it was just so *wonderful* that such a *wonderful*
    man had found any time at all for her —
And Doddis softens —
(and Sammy will move in with Doddis, together the better
    to keep bright the Captain's memory.)

The reading of the will had its moment —
the Captain had left his effects variously between Doddis, and
    Sammy, and the Venus in Furs —
but with this proviso: that were it to chance that the three of
    them all snuffed it within six months of the reading of the
    will —
in that event, another envelope must be opened —
'Paul!' I said, 'What a Dad! What a funeral! —
I wouldn't have missed that for anything! —
We must keep in touch!' —
And I waved him off on the plane back to Toronto.

Six months later I was watching the first run of *The Exor-*
    cist —
Remember it? —
The Exorcist begins with an archaeological dig —
'Northern Iraq' it says, and there's a bunch of Arabs digging —
    and then there's the call to prayer —
And then we're snaking through the archaeological site with
    the little Arab boy —
Boy suddenly stops and through his spread little Arab legs

we see Max von Sydow —
And Max is portraying the archaeological site facilitator —
(the Sheik Fixit if you like) —
And the little boy's saying in Arabic (there are subtitles):
'They've found something!' —
Now with the Arab archaeologist, and he is saying to Max:
　'Some interesting finds. Lamps, arrowheads, coins.' —
MAX (*examining some crap*): 'Strange . . . not of the same
　period' —
Max, scrabbling up crevice pulls out appalling object —
too appalling for us to be allowed to look at properly yet —
Cut to the café —
It's two hours later
(Two hours later! —
Max von Sydow has aged twenty years!) —
Max is on heart tablets now —
And then we're in that little museum —
in heavy Arab company, talking Arabic —
'Shatan', we hear the word: 'Shatan' —
'Evil against evil,' we read —
Max is fiddling with another (or the same) appalling object
　which stops the clock! —
Heavy Arab says, 'I wish you didn't have to go' —
MAX: 'There is something I must do.'

Now driving towards archaeological site —
Halted by Arabs in flowing white robes with guns —
(Arabs relax a bit when they see it's Max)
Max allowed onto site —
And that's when you see it! —
Maybe you glimpsed it before —
but not like this! —

the dog-dragon statue! —
And there's wild dogs fighting themselves to death down there —
and then there's the Sun going down behind the statue —
(Ugh!) —
The statue! —
Max! —
Statue! —
Max! —

Cut to Georgetown, USA.

That line: 'There is something I must do' is redundant in
   the movie —
in fact it's confusing —
What did Max von Sydow have to do? —
Go and watch the sun go down on a statue? —
Or does it refer to his book, maybe? —
Do you remember the plot of the thing? —
Once we've left the desert, we're in Georgetown, USA, and
   it's all about this little American girl and how her head keeps
   twiddling right round, and she can't stop spitting green stuff
   at vicars —
Then someone says, 'Hey – we haven't seen Max von Sydow
   for nearly an hour now —
Let's go and see what he's doing —
Maybe he could help!' —
And we find Max, now living in Woodstock, USA and in
   the middle of writing a book —
And so that's what he must have meant by 'There is something
   I must do':

'I must just watch the sun set on that statue, and then get out of here, maybe rent a cottage in somewhere like Woodstock and write a book'.

I was on the phone to Paul in Toronto —
'Have you seen *The Exorcist?*' —
He said, 'Yeah man I have. And listen: that was the Captain's dig!' —
"Northern Iraq?" Bollocks! —
The whole thing was shot in Muskat, Oman' —
That the Captain was working for *The Exorcist* film company as well as for Doddis —
He was batting round Oman in a helicopter finding locations for them —
That Max von Sydow bases his characterization on Captain Charlie Charrington —
Those are actually the Captain's heart tablets in the café scene! —
And that museum you see there, that's Kontardi's museum! —
And it was a party for *The Exorcist* film crew and company, when they'd all wanted him to stay, but the captain had said: '*No, there is something I must do*' —
and had gone off into the desert with his old friend —
and to his death —
And that his death had been unspeakably weirder than a heart attack —
that Doris Kontardi had had to spread a lot of money around Muskat to buy that certificate —
and be permitted to fly her Captain back to England —
And that line, 'There is something I must do,' is in that film as a mark of respect and love for Captain Charlie Charrington.

I would suggest that there is a hole in the plotting of *The Exorcist*:
How did the appalling object get from Northern Iraq to the
  bottom of some stairs in Georgetown, USA?

Were you with me in my kitchen now, I would be introducing
  you to this 'old friend' —

This Dog-dragon figurine (9″) —
You'd note the Dog-dragon snouting —
(and that this snouting would be even more impressive if it
hadn't been part snapped-off somewhere in its history) —
And the cloak-cum-wing effect there at the back —
I would suggest to you that had we the magic of movie effects
we could put the breeze up folk with this thing as effectively
as the one in *The Exorcist* —
And I can tell you how this got to the bottom of my garden —
(Haverstock Hill, 1981) —
It was like this:
I was directing the Czech comedy *War with the Newts* at the
Riverside Studios Hammersmith and we'd broken rehearsals
for the day and I was passing Olympia —
And on at Olympia now was the 'Mind and Body' Exhibition —
the 'New Age' effort —
and there'd been some humour there in previous years, so
I decided to potter in —
But actually it was rather tacky that year —
There was a MacDonald's —
and I found the whole thing doubtful —
e.g. crystal pendulums —
just expensive things on strings really —
but you'd be able to find lost stuff with them was the claim —
they start twiddling the other way round when you near your
lost thing —
And buried treasure too! —
All you need do is DANGLE IT OVER A MAP and it'll
jerk about when it's over anything interesting —
What bollocks! —
And this dame offering to look sideways into the iris of your
eyes, and prescribe exactly what stuff you ought to be sniffing
in order to release your potential —
Three Rotherham Buddhists insisting if you chant 'Nam Yoho
Bother Um' several hours a morning and eat and drink

nothing but carrot for a month you wouldn't have any more
problems —
Bollocks —
and dangerous bollocks! —
But I was halted by the last stall to the left of the exit —
which was a stall of magic wands . . .
Not the kind of wand a stage conjuror would use —
These were 'Earth Magic Wands for Successful Magic':

*'Wands must always be culled at dawn or dusk, when the
Sun's rays strike the trees from the side and not from above.
And it gives a marvellous feeling to be in a deep wood at first
light with all the trees excitedly jostling about you, offering their
branches for magical use. In minutes my arms are full and I
have to decline the rest as gracefully as possible so as not to
cause offence.'*

These wands (and very weird they were) are individually hand-
crafted by the stall proprietor Dusty Miller —
'These wands,' I found myself asking Mr Miller, 'would they
be useful in the directing of Czechoslovakian comedy?' —
'Is that what you do?' he said —
'Well, it's what I'm doing at the moment,' I said —
He said, 'More than likely' —
I said, 'Well could you steer me to a wand that might be
useful for that purpose then?' —
'No,' he said, 'I can't do that. I can't do that because you
have to let the wand choose you.' —
So I stood in front of all these wands —
Seeing if one wanted me —
And there was this really *wicked* wand, and I was thinking,
'Go on! You have me!' —
But it went all queeny on me —
'No,' it was saying. 'No-oo' (campily) —
But the one that seemed to have its eye (!) on me . . .
I guess we've all popped along to the zoo in springtime in

order to see a baboon's erection? —
The first erection of spring? —
When it's pencil thin with the wonger on the top? —
And when they first notice them, these baboons, they don't
    know what they're for —
They ping them at each other —
They think perhaps they've been summoned to some sort of
    novelty conker tournament —
It's not until they've got the mauve bots that they know what
    they're for . . .
But this is not going to turn into a David Attenborough
    evening —
What I wanted to say was that the wand that wanted me
    was like a male baboon's donger in early May —
'P'raps that one,' I said, pointing —
'Hmmm,' said Dusty, 'could be a match —
But look, about these wands —
Do try and keep it with you at all times, at least for the first
    month – until we find out whether it gets on with you or not.' —
And if it didn't get on with me, he'd give me my five pounds
    back, or exchange it for another wand —
I left with it inside my jacket —
Out, it would have excited comment —
possibly arrest.

Lurking outside the Olympia portals was an old chum, Richard
    Kilgour, composer —
But the reason he was there was because a couple of weeks
    before, he'd parted with £250 to the Silva Mind Control
    outfit who had a stall in the Exhibition —
The Silva Mind Control, Kilgour tells me, train you up in a
    system called 'Dream Mirroring' —
and if you apply yourself fully to that for some weeks, you

find that you've so tuned your mind up that you only have
to visualize something and you get it —
'Well for £250 Richard,' I said, 'that's a snip if it really works —
Oh look,' I said. (A poster.) 'Bob Dylan's on at Earl's Court
tonight —
Shall we go and see Bob Dylan?' —
'No,' he said. 'We wouldn't get in. It'll be all booked up' —
I said, 'Actually we might – I've got a magic wand,' (giving
him a peek at the beast) —
'Oh,' he said. 'Well it'd be a handy opportunity for me to
try out my visualizing' —
And so off to Earl's Court, and a battle of the sorcerers:
Richard takes up position on the corner of side road opposite
Earls Court, eyes upwards behind lids, awful bit of eye-white
beneath pupil showing —
and humming pottily, attempts visualization of Bob Dylan
tickets —
I go on to next road, wait till moment is right —
Out with naughty wand! Waving!!
'Two tickets Bob Dylan!'
and this fellow comes running up —
sold me two tickets —
I said, 'I'll give you another fiver if you take these two tickets
and give them to that man with his eyes shut over there! —
If he says anything, don't say anything back! —
just come on like you're a deaf mute or something! Hubba
bubba hubba bubba!'
Chap agrees.

Richard comes over to me with the tickets. He is *shaken* —
'Wow man!' he said. 'I'd just got them visualized and this
spastic came up to me and thrusts them at me!' —
Even weirder, being only a junior in the Silva Mind Control, he

hadn't liked to bother the aetheric with anything excessive, so
he'd only dared to visualize back row seats —
And that's exactly what he got!

Once in Earl's Court, I had the wand out and proud —
And this fellow came running up to me and he said: 'Can
   I see your ticket?' —
I said: 'Certainly' —
'Oo,' he said. 'That's a crappy ticket! —
You can sit with me, my friend hasn't come' —
And so we went with this guy (me and the wand) —
second row seats us, Bob Dylan —
Richard had to go to the back —
It was all he'd visualized —
I thought, Wow, this wand likes me! It gets on with me! —
I slept with it, of course, and the next morning was Sunday —
and I thought: I'll clear my shed out today, and I put the
   wand on the window ledge of the shed to supervise —
and I was humping stuff out of the shed and I kept passing,
   embedded in the lawn, what I took to be my little daughter
   Daisy's upturned chalk boat —
I thought, What chalk boat? She hasn't got a chalk boat! —
And then I thought: – I don't think I've ever seen a chalk boat —
I pringed it out of the lawn, and it was this Dog-dragon figurine —
The moment I picked it up, I saw clearly in my mind's eye —
(I rationalize that it's *The Exorcist* connection) —
the dashing phiz of Captain Charlie Charrington —
I chummed the figurine with the wand on the window ledge —
At first I took it to be a novelty chess piece – that was
   my theory —
I assumed the neighbours had been playing novelty chess —
and got so pissed off with it they'd hurled the novelty chess
   pieces about the gardens —

But as the day wore on I knew it was no novelty chess piece,
    this —
I thought: I'd really like to show this to Dusty Miller —
And it was the last day of the Mind and Body Exhibition —
I sped back to Olympia —
'Mr Miller,' I said, 'two tickets for Bob Dylan, that's one thing —
But what do you make of this?' —
and showed him the Dog-dragon —
He took it —
He held it professionally —
He said, 'Well I don't think it means *you* any harm —
But if I were you I'd have it checked out by the Black Magic
    artefact couple over there —' —
Who turned out to be an hysterical pair —
They were Whoopsie people —
And they bred enormous snakes and had a coven in Willesden
    every Thursday —
And they offered to whoopsie off with the Dog-dragon and
    get the next Thursday's coven to psychometrize it and find
    out more about it —
And I thought, Well how exciting, yeah okay —
But the coven uncovered nothing —
And so they took it to the British Museum —
And the British Museum said, 'Well we don't know what it is —
We think it was made in perhaps the late 1700s —
but for what purpose we really couldn't tell you' —
Meanwhile, Dusty Miller said, 'When you get back see if there
    are any more —
Sometimes when you find one, you find more' —
I hadn't got a lot of faith in that actually —
And it was dusk when the wand and I got back,
and I thought I knew this little bit of garden, but —
whoopsie —
I saw it almost right away —
A little pyramid of white coming up through the lawn —
And I got a trowel and dug it up with extreme care —

And it was this: Exhibit Two: the Pair of Legs (5″) —

Draped legs —
Or maybe they're legs behind a curtain —
And then the next day, I found the Shrieking Monk top half
   (4″) —

for many the freakiest of the set —
This loop of wire in the mouth . . . —
What is that? —

Presumably he's shrieking: 'Coul' sonhwonh ge' 'is fu' wire
ou' o' 'y 'ou', 'lease!' —
Sometimes people think that the Shrieking Monk belongs to
the Legs —
Honestly, we think it's doubtful —
He doesn't fit them —
But also, if you had his loop-of-wire-in-the-mouth problem,
it's unlikely that you'd be standing quite like *that* —
and the Legs on their own are sinister —
the Monk top half, ghastly —
But stick them together and it's a silly whoopsie man —
'What a beautiful day, brothers, for putting a loop of wire
in your mouth, doing a whoopsie behind the curtain, and
shouting "Wire (why're) we slaves of our habits?!" '

'FOKWAEA' is a Pidgin word —
(Pidgin English – the language of the South Pacific) —
I first came on the word in the phrase 'Bigman Jif blong
    Fokwaea Aelan' —
'Aelan' means 'island'; 'Bigman Jif' is the 'chief' – or 'squire'
    we might say —
'blong' here is 'of' —
So: 'The Squire of Fokwaea Island' —
'Fokwaea' (note the influence of Irish on Pidgin here) is 'barbed
    wire'!

In the cast of *Warp*, the World's Longest Play, (see Guinness
    Book of Records years 1981, 1982, 1983) which I directed,
    we had the services of young actor David DeNil —*
And David DeNil was the most minimal person I have ever
    encountered —
I will recall for you how he used to smoke a cigarette:
There would be barely sufficient energy in those fingers to
    hold the cigarette —
any less, and the fag would have dropped on the carpet —
And the lips too: minimal energy there —
And his walk was such that it caused minimum alarm to insect
    life —
I couldn't have him do too much in the show, because apart
    from all that, he was totally inaudible —
'I suppose there's no chance of you speaking up David?!!' —

*The video of the original *Warp* production – all 18 hours of it, plus some other novelties Neil has
bunged on for the seeker – may be purchased for £100 (plus P & P) from the author: Neil Oram,
Goshem, Grotaig, Bunloit Road, Near Drumnadrochil, Invernessshire, Scotland.

What can't you hear me? —
'No, we can't hear **anything**!' —
But I found a remarkable use for the guy, because it turned
    out that he had the legendary Minus Quality —
i.e., if he left the room, the stage looked somehow fuller —
And it was a terrific way of starting off a scene —
You'd have David leave —
and it was like turning up the pink light.

Anyway, what I want to tell you: the show was up and running,
    and a sensation —
And I'd gone to bed and I was asleep and I'd started to dream —
And then this chap *barged into my dream*, and he said:
'You know that David DeNil feller who's in your production?' —
I said, 'Yes?' . . . He said, 'What he's got to do is this:
He's got to go and see every live show that Ken Dodd gives
    for a year —
Will you tell him?' —
I said, 'Yes, alright,' and then he left and I was allowed to
    get on with my dream —
And I went flying I think, and whatnot —
But then this dream wound up in the South Pacific —
and my late mother was roped to a window sill —
and I was just cutting her free, when this chap turned up again —
He said, 'You won't forget to tell David, will you?' —
I said, 'I'm just rescuing my mother!' —
But this chap and his demands were in my mind when I woke
    up in a way that I think no dream should ever be —
(I don't think it's healthy) —
When I went into the theatre that evening, there was David —
He was minimally applying his make-up —
He wasn't due on for an hour yet —
for his first exit —

'Ah David,' I said. 'I had a dream about you last night —
In fact I was instructed as to what you've got to do with
　　your future —
I don't know what you think about these things, but it seems
　　to me that if you ask me what it was, then you've got to do
　　it —
But if you don't, you won't' —
And David said, 'Thank you' —
And he didn't ask me! —
Until we got to the pub, and he said, 'What is it I've got to do?' —
'What you've got to do David, is see every live show that
　　Ken Dodd gives for a year.' —
'Thank you,' said David —
And then later he said: Would it be alright if I don't start till January?' —
I said I thought January would be fine —
And January saw him taking off to Southport —
He hadn't got much money, so he borrowed an arctic sleeping-
　　bag —
and he slept on Southport beach under the pier —
Doddy was doing his pantomime there —
David was on the beach for more than a week —
until he made some minimal friends who let him sleep on
　　their floor —
He showed the box office manageress what little money he'd
　　got, and she gave him a serial ticket so he could see all the
　　shows —
That's twice daily —
three times on a Wednesday —
three times on a Saturday —
And he didn't miss any of them! —
And then he got two weeks off —
And then Ken Dodd was doing a tour of cities and towns
　　of the North of England —
David kept with that tour; didn't miss one performance, and
　　at the end of the tour, Ken Dodd has a little party on the
　　stage —

And David DeNil has the courage not only to attend the
party, but go up and introduce himself to Ken Dodd, and
tell the man what he's doing —
i.e., his intention is to see every live show Doddy gives for
a year —
And that this was down to a dream which a friend of his
had had —
Ken Dodd said: 'Well David, I think you may have problems
with my next engagement.'
David asked why —
And Dodd said, 'Because it's in the New Hebrides: F-Farty!' —
And when Dodd said 'F-Farty!' David took this to be some
Scouse expression meaning 'Be off with you!' —
But David couldn't see what the problem was going to be —
He'd got the date of this gig, and presumably he'd have to
apply himself in good time to the relevant Scottish ferry —
But then he couldn't find the *New* Hebrides on the map —
Up there by Scotland, there's Outer Hebrides and Inner Heb-
rides, but no *New* Hebrides —
For the New Hebrides you turn left at Fiji —
And the capital of the New Hebrides is Efaté Island —
And David ran —
My expression meaning David would now do anything for
money —
Anything!! —
And he knocked it up, he knocked up the required sum —
And we waved him goodbye —
Off to Efaté Island —
Flying by way of Sydney, Australia —
And we got a postcard back from David —
and it seemed it was quite a lark on Efaté Island —
He'd met some very nice Australians —
he'd also been interviewing gentlemen with feathers in their
noses —
But listen, he'd been to the yacht club, he'd been to the
three hotels, he'd been to all the bars —

And nobody had heard of Ken Dodd!

But David was to become famous on Efaté Island as the Man
    Looking For Ken Dodd —
He knew all the gags, he knew all the routines —
People would say, 'Well who is this Ken Dodd then?' —
And David could go on till next morning —
The language spoken on Efaté Island, and on all the islands
    of the New Hebrides (now the Republic of Vanuatu), and in
    the Solomon Islands, and Papua New Guinea, and more —
the inter-island language, the *lingua franca*, is Pidgin English —
This is no more than 1,500 words of English (quaintly mutated
    and oddly spelled) —
but with cunning, you can steer them to almost any concept —
And it only takes about a week to pick up Pidgin, and David
    was now amusing himself by translating Ken Dodd's routines
    into Pidgin for the entertainment of the natives —
And there was a bunch of natives and they were going to be
    canoeing off the next morning to visit their more primitive
    cousins on Ambrym and Malekula, and on to the Solomon
    Islands —
They wondered if David would like to come with them —
'Oo yes please' —
On Malekula the chaps had their bollocks swinging free but
    their pricks in wrappers —
they were soon informed that tonight was to be a special
    evening —
the sort of evening you'd really got to tog up for —
So they hummed away the afternoon, painting their legs up,
    putting on their clankers and sticking their danglers in —
And then when they were sat about under the banyan tree
    they were all introduced to David DeNil —
And David DeNil launched into the first gag of his Pidgin

Dodd routine —
And the Bigman Chief of the Island called for him to halt —
and go back and tell it again —
And then halt, and go back and tell it again —
And he told it five times —
But on the fifth time of telling the whole Island held its sides
and howled away the night in laughter! —
And the next day he was canoed on to the next island —
Listen, he toured nineteen islands with one gag! —
And this is it:

> 'Im fulugud dei. Im fulugud dei blong yumitufala
> pushem lilfala salwata wanae
> insaed postofis letahol blong praeafala pasta
> talim – "ski aelan twinki twink plantifala ia!" '

You'll notice that David took a liberty with Dodd's text here:
'Lilfala salwata wanae' —
that's because there aren't actually cucumbers as such on the
islands —
I'm sure you could probably steer your way, circumnavigate
Pidgin and arrive at the concept of cucumberishness —
But it could take all afternoon —
For example the word for piano is:
'Bigfala bokis blong Waetman; tut blong im – sam i blak,
sam i waet – yu kilim emi singaot' —
Bokis = box; tut = teeth —
Kilim isn't 'kill,' it's only 'hit'. —
If you want to say 'kill', you have to say: 'Kilim altageta
ded finis yeah!' —

Doddy's song Love is Like a Violin would come out as,
'Lavem laekem lilfala bokis – sipos yu skrasem beli – emi
kraeout' —

So for cucumber David took the easy way out, and went for
   the '*lilfala salwata wanae*' concept —
'Little fellow salt water one-eye' —
And actually not such a little fellow —
you might encounter one whilst paddling off a Solomon Island —
It's a species of Solomon Island sea slug —
If you do see one, whip it out the water – they're long brown
   things with a luminous green streak —
Whip it out, and give it a clout and it'll cough up a bit of
   khaki unpleasantness and then go limp —
and you can toss it onto the beach and it'll dry out, and you
   can grind it up and make a fishy pepper to sprinkle on your
   yams.

David's gag would come in one of Doddy's 'What a beautiful
   day' routines.
'What a beautiful day for running into Woolworths and shouting:
   "Tescos"!' —
'What a beautiful day for putting your kilt on upside down,
   standing on your head and shouting: "How's that for a shuttle-
   cock!" ' —
So —
Im fulugud dei – What a beautiful day —
blong – for ('blong' is all the prepositions)
yumitufala – we, us (lit. 'You-me-two-fellows')
pushem lilfala salwata wanae – to shove a little salt water
   one-eyed chappy
insaed postofis letahol – into the letterbox
blong praeafala pasta – belonging to the vicar

talim – '*ski aelan twinki twink plantifala ia!*' – tell him 'the
 sky island twinkle twinkle people are here!'
Dodd's original: 'What a beautiful day for shoving a cucumber
 in the vicar's letterbox and shouting: "The Martians have
 arrived!" '

David's also locally revered as the fala who introduced Limerick
 form to the islands —
This I think is one of his best efforts:

'Runemfala flaengfokis
Bol defren habig, no mokis!
Wan bol smol
Nomo no bol,
Narafala bigfala: winim praes bokis':

runemfala – a hunter (with a spear) —
flaeng fokis – flying fox —
bol – 'ball', or 'balls'. (They don't bother with S's for plurals
 out there – you have to know it by context. I happen to know
 that in this case it's 'balls'.)
Habig – size, sizes (lit. 'how big') —
bol defren habig – balls of different sizes —
No mokis – no laughter! —
Wan bol smol – one ball small —
Nomo no bol – almost no ball —
Narafala – the other one —
bigfala – a big one —
Winim praes bokis – wins him prize boxes —
(It's always the same prize every year on the Solomon Islands,
but they pay a great deal of attention to the mud-and-wicker
 box it comes in) —
David, probably recalling there the young sport from Devizes —

'. . . Whose balls were of different sizes,
One ball was small,
Almost no ball at all,
But the other was large and won prizes.'

But I think the more enchanting in David's Pidgin.

According to David, the rudest word on the islands is *'hambag'* —
which means unnatural unsanctioned sex with an underage girl
  to whose father you haven't given six pigs —
Apparently the British Council had funded Dame Edith Evans
  to do her one woman favourite snippets show round the
  islands —
The first clanger might have been that women performing at all
  is contrary to custom, but they'd thought she was a bloke —
But when she'd given her *Importance of Being Earnest* she'd
  had to canoe for it —

Anyway, we learn all this sort of thing when David at length
  returns from his Solomon Islands adventure —
His greeting is strange:
he doesn't shake your hand, or kiss you or anything usual —
he grabs you by the upper arm and gives it a squeeze —
And evidently that is a Solomon Islands greeting —
a throwback to the good old days —
(They were eating each other on a regular basis up until about
  1935) —
And apparently the upper arm is the second tastiest part of
  a person —

So the greeting means literally: 'Hmmm . . . so far so good
   . . . like to know you better!' —
And another thing: David is no longer minimal —
This dates from his falling in love on the islands —
It's not only feathers they put in their noses —
they put all sorts of stuff there: pencils, pens, cigarettes, cigars —
But David had, on the island of Ambrym encountered the
   apprentice priestess of some cargo cult —
and she'd so worked on her nasal cartilage that she could
   snap it over items like soup tins, harpic containers —
and play them —
(make a good novelty act with the Bishop, that) —
But David was in a bit of a dilemma: —
Was he **really** in love with her? —
or was he merely in love with the idea of introducing her
   to his mother? —
Either way, he realized it was all up now with his minimalism.

David handed me a properly made out bill —
invoicing me for £3,000; I said, 'Good Lord, what's this
   David?' —
He said, 'Well, look I didn't fulfil your commission as
   worded —
– i.e., I didn't go and see every live show that Ken Dodd
   gave for a year —
But bringing all this stuff back, doesn't it open some doors
   for you?' —
'Yes,' I said. 'Yes David, maybe it does —
But there's no sense in which I *commissioned* you to do
   anything —
I merely had the goodness to tell you what some geezer
   who barged into my dream *told* me to tell you' —
'Yeah,' he said, and he was going round my place picking

stuff up —
not like he was looking for clues —
it was more like he had all the evidence he required —
He had plans for returning to the islands, he said —
probably offering himself for the hundred day circumcision
    ritual —
and then thus cleansed, claiming the trainee priestess —
(She wasn't just somewhere to stick your old tins —
she was a loving, caring woman —
And his for six pigs! —)
'There's homosexuality on the islands,' he said —
'O,' I said. 'Well there's homosexuality here, I believe.' —
'Yes,' he said, 'but here it's optional.'
And as he was leaving he turned to me and said:
'So carry on up your own arsehole then' —
And he was gone —
And I thought, Wow – that's a really big man's just gone
    out of here —
And I really experienced envy —
I really envied him his journey —
how far he'd got —
what he might do next —
The Bigman Jif blong Fokwaea Aelan . . .

The Melvyn Bragg Show once took a passing interest in my
   Two-Faced Acting Classes —
And I still do them —

but now I call it my Enantiodromic Approach to Drama —
and charge a lot more money for it —
The Enantiodromic Approach is simply the study of how one
    side of the face is different from the other —
They're different people —
You can look at one side of a chap's face and say, 'It's the
    face of a serial killer' —
and then you look at the other and it's got something of
    Mother Theresa about it —
And the answer is of course that it's both —
A face is composed of two contradictory, mutually exclusive
    facets —
And my Enantiodromic classes help you stress your contra-
    dictions —
Under laboratory scrutiny, it seems that my right facet is that
    of a vacant inept housewife called Elsie —
And the left side is my Spanking Squire side —
The Spanking Squire —
he's into the chastisement of the young ladies of the village
    whether they've been naughty or not —
I find this is useful knowledge not only in performing but in life —
encountering real people —
When meeting women for the first time, I know to present
    them with my Elsie side —
I mumble and burble through her, and they're really much
    happier with that —
It's not till much later in the relationship that I play my Spanking
    Squire!

When I do this as a live show it's about now that I sense a
    rumble in the house of what I call 'stage property angst' —
I schlepp about with me quite a load of gear —
on the stage with me will be my photo of Stuart Pearce;

Dog-dragon, Monk and Legs; the complete paperback works
of Philip K. Dick; a map of London with pins in it; a ball of
wool; mouldering 10″ × 8″ of the Fuck-The-Hell Bar; Ken
Dodd's routines in Pidgin on big boards; tickling sticks; a
curly brim bowler; ladies' clothes and wig; and more —
As I move through my subjects I move through my objects —
the props serving to both authenticate and prompt —
It's my Doddis museum —
an extension of the Gearies Friday Showtime —
and there are these three major items I haven't mentioned yet:
    Balinese Wooden Frog and Umbrella carving (4½′) —
    Fur Bugs Bunny Disguised in toad mask (5′) —
    And a Melanesian Ken Dodd Idol (4½′) —
The Melanesian Dodd is such a sensation that it is in disguise —
It's wearing a Papua New Guinea wartyfala mask —
and I don't reveal its true identity till the very end of the show —
anyway, if I've sensed the 'property angst' —
that people think they've tumbled how the show works now —
'He's got to go round and he's got to pick everything up
    and he's got to show us it all before we can go home' —
then I'll get a load of things handled and out of the way —
For example, the three big items, I'll explain, simply tell us
    that this is part of a trilogy —
The first part was *Furtive Nudist*, sometimes called *The Recollec-
tions of a Furtive Nudist* – and the logo, the three dimensional
totem of *Furtive Nudist* was the Frog —
'Here's tonight's gent,' I say, drawing attention to the Melanesian
    Doddy in warty masquerade —
'featured mascot of *Pigspurt – or Six Pigs from Happiness*' —
'And this' – (Bugs Bunny) – 'will be the totem of part three,
    Jamais Vu —
One predicts that at the climax of *Jamais Vu* when I remove
    the toad mask' —
– (doing so) —
'revealing Bugs Bunny, —
there won't be a dry seat in the house'.

Do you know the expression 'jamais vu'? —
Well 'déjà vu' – English expression, French words —
Déjà vu is when you arrive somewhere you've never been
before and think: *I've been here before* . . .
Jamais vu is when you go home, and you say *Christ I've
never been here before!* —
I will of course be dealing with jamais vu in its extreme form —
That's when you go home, say *Christ I've never been here
before and I'm not even here now!* —
There was a stirring case of jamais vu last year in Scotland —
A Dundee girl had jamais vu on her father —
Father came in from work and she thought: *That's not my
father!* —
She had jamais vu on him, you see —
And she came to the opinion that he was an android —
And to prove the point she pulled his throat out to expose
the wires! —
And she was wrong —
It may not have been her father, I don't know, but it certainly
wasn't a robot —
And of course Derek —
Derek and his mum who chopped him up —
Possibly a case of jamais vu there.

People think, Oh Christ he's going to have to read all those
books to us! —
But no no no. This is just my collection of the works of
the late American author Philip K. Dick —

That's because I'm what is known in science fiction circles
   as a 'Dickhead' —
We Dickheads are divided into two camps —
There are those who'll tell you: 'Only read the books he wrote
   before 1974, all the later stuff's crap!' —
And then there are the others who'll say, 'No no no —
It's the ones after '74, they're the ones! —
Get into them ones and don't bother with the rest!'
   Why this unhealthy schism? —
It's because it was in 1974 that Philip K. Dick had the pink
   light experience —
Whether Philip K. Dick did in fact encounter the Almighty —
Or whether it was something else —
Sometimes he writes of it as 'being bathed in living
   knowledge' . . .
The title of that post-74 work 'VALIS', is an acronym for
   Vast Active Living Intelligence System —
And chum, I've got this: *The Selected Letters of Philip K.
   Dick 1974* —
i.e., only the letters that he wrote the year of the pink light —
And it's £39.95, and quite right – that'll keep the wankers off it —
If you're Philip K. Dickering, this one's probably a good start:
Divine Invasions – A Life of Philip K. Dick by Lawrence Sutin —
Lawrence Sutin's an American who knew Dick in the last
   few years of his life —
And wonderfully he flew over to be with us at the annual
   East London Dickheads Convention —
And it was Lawrence who told us about Philip K. Dick *and
   the snuff* —
Evidently Dick was into snuff in a big way —
(He was a big man, with a beard) —
And he'd be regaling the lads with new theories —
as to what the fuck had happened to him in 1974, u.s.w. —
And he'd have all these tins of snuff ranged in front of him —
about nine or ten tins in different flavours —
snuff comes in different flavours! —

And he'd be going from one tin of snuff to another —
amazing the guys —
And Lawrence described Dick as being 'covered in snizz' —
I'd never seen my hero in that light before —
Covered in snizz. Wow! —
And I thought, Well if I'm ever going to excite the seekers
    to anything like the degree that Dick has excited me, I've
    probably got to get into snuff —
I thought it'd be kinda nifty if after my death, people would say:
'Did you ever actually see him? Did you ever see Campbell?'
And they'd say, 'Yeah yeah, I did' —
'Wow, what was he like?' —
'Well, he was . . . covered in snizz!' —
And of course if you really want to get into anything, you
    discover it's just round the corner —
and been there for years —
In the newsagent Patel's they'd been grinding up snuff for
    years —
and they'd grind up any flavour you like —
I found that menthol, mentholated snuff was my chap —
Listen: throw away the fags! throw away the Havanas, boys! —
Snuff! —
That is the BIG ONE! —
And I was in my local, the Anchor and Hope*, demonstrating
    to Les the landlord the art of snuff-taking —
when into the bar came our local star: Buster Bloodvessel,
    leader of the Bad Manners pop group —
And Buster's like the Laughing Buddha on one side —
and like Boris Karloff in *Grip of the Strangler* on the other —
Buster entered the bar enantiodromically, and for humour he
    went:
'AAAAHHH **TCHOOOO**!' in my snuff tin —
Blasted all the snuff everywhere! —
'I'll have to get some more now!' (posing as amused) —

---

*See *Furtive Nudist* by Ken Campbell (Methuen) pp. 66–7, 78 and 83.

But not to worry —
because that day, Buster had this little run-around boy who
    was doing everything for him – any little errand – on a BMX
    bike —
And so I told the lad to go round to Patel's —
and to be sure to get it ground up with the menthol —
And I gave him the right money.

A long time later I learned this:
That the little lad had spent some of my money on comics,
    and bought some bubblegum —
so he got lightweight of snuff —
On the way back, I guess he was a wee bit worried about
    this —
So, passing a dried up dog turd of similar hue he snapped
    the tip off and crumbled it into the bag —
I just innocently funnelled it into my tin —
And then snuffled up a couple of pinches —
I said: 'Les, have you had an incontinent dog in here? —
I think a dog's shit somewhere . . .' —
'I can't smell anything,' says Les —
I said, 'Well clear your nose with this then' —
And he said: 'It's good stuff that! I've got it now' —
And Buster's drummer comes in, and sees Les and me sniffing
    around on our hands and knees —
He says: 'What are you guys doing down there?' —
Les said: 'There's a dog shit somewhere!' —
'I can't smell it,' says Drummer —
'Clear his nose, Ken,' says Les . . .

When I got home, I felt a bit Philip K. Dicky —
And you know how you go into the bathroom, to see if you're
    ill? —
I was looking in the mirror —
and I thought, No no – we're alright. There's Elsie, there's
    the Spanking Squire —
We're all present and correct —
And then I had a revelation —
Back to the pub: 'Buster! Boys! Look at my nose! —
Try and divorce my nose from the rest of my face! What
    does it remind you of?' —
And Buster said, 'Smugglers' coves! With 'orrible stalagmites!' —
'What?' I said. 'No no – not the nostrils —
Be looking more at the body of the nose . . .'
But they couldn't get anything —
I said, 'Look, is it not a naked lady from the rear? —
There's the cleavage of her buttocks at the end —
And there's her thighs – a wee bit spread —
And you can't see her hair because she's washing it.' —
And they got it —
'Yeah yeah. It's quite a turn on, your nose, as it happens' —
(There was tasteless humour about the pubes —
which has made me self-conscious about my nasal hair —
I trim the stuff every morning —
and keep the clippings in a jar.) —
Buster's drummer, he's got kids, and (giving me dolls' house
    sofa) he said, 'Here you are Ken! Something for her to sit
    on! Ah hah haahhh!' —
When I got home, I was doing my Stuart Pearce impressions:
'*A knife in the back . . . is not what we call . . . a normal
    death, CARSTAIRS!*' —
There was a knock at the door – it was Buster —
And Buster had had a vision. 'It's Cinderella, Ken!' he said.
    'It's a Cinderella fing!' —
I said, 'What is?' He said, 'Your nose is: – it's Cinderella
    and the slipper! —

What you've got to do, you've got to comb the land for her
   whose arse matches your nose —
and then *slip her one!*' —
'I've got a song coming on,' he said, and left.

It was just a silliness to begin with —
People would come round, get a bit pissed —
I'd get the Polaroid out: 'Will it be you my dear?' —
I don't think it would have gone any further than that —
if it hadn't been for the coming of Dick's *Exegesis* —
Philip K. Dick – a prolific man. He wrote forty novels before
   1974 —
then there was the pink light and he only wrote four* —
But he wasn't being lazy —
Every day he was at the typewriter —
often typing through the night —
But mostly this stuff wasn't for publication —
It was like letters —
but not letters *to* anybody —
Letters maybe to the very depths of himself —
And he called this stuff his *Exegesis* —
And when he died, he left behind about four million words
   in bundles and boxes —
and Lawrence Sutin had now read it all, and Lawrence sent me:
Selections from the Exegesis – the first published fragments
   of the legendary *Exegesis* of Dick† —
And Lawrence warned me that you couldn't get into this one
   unless you'd first read his selected significant terms at the
   back, the glossary —
'Otherwise you won't be able to make head or tail of it,' he said —

Valis, The Divine Invasion, The Transmigration of Timothy Archer, Radio Free Albemuth.

†*In Pursuit of Valis – Selections from the Exegesis* edited by Lawrence Sutin, published by Underwood-Miller, Novato, California 1991.

And that's where I found 'Enantiodromia' —

> '*Enantriodromia*: the sudden transformation into an opposite
> form or tendency. The term was used by Heraclitus, but PKD
> [Dick] first became familiar with it through his reading of C.G.
> Jung . . .'

So there we are: I'm only the fourth person to use it, I guess —
Heraclitus, then Jung, then Dick, then me —
And on the next page is 'Pigspurt' —
It says: '*Pigspurt*: see *Plasmate*' —
Not an awfully difficult thing to do because *Plasmate* is the
next word.

> '*Plasmate*: Literally *living* knowledge. PKD often felt that
> he had bonded with it in 2-3-74,† and that, as a result, there
> dwelled within his psyche what seemed to be a *second* entirely
> other self . . . At times, Dick believed that the identity of this
> second self was the late James A. Pike . . .'

(Incidentally Bishop Pike, the heretical bishop of California
who came to believe that Jesus was a mushroom) —

> '. . . with whom PKD had been friends in the mid-1960s. At
> other times, he posited an early Christian named Thomas . . .'

blah blah blah – Here we go! —

> '. . . Yet another identity posed by PKD was Pigspurt, a
> malevolent force that had filled him with fear and a craven
> attitude toward governmental authority; but it should be noted
> that Pigspurt was seldom mentioned – PKD rarely regarded
> this second self as malevolent. As for the plasmate itself, he
> most often regarded it as the living transmission of the Gnostic
> goddess Saint Sophia, Holy Wisdom. Another name coined by
> Dick for this Holy Wisdom was Firebright.'

---

*2-3-74 is Dick's shorthand term for his pink light experiences of February through March, 1974.

I thought, well one thing's for sure: I'm going to nick this
  word 'Enantiodromia' —
at that moment was born a nice little earner —
The Enantiodromic Approach to Drama! —
But it occurred to me, that maybe I ought to tart up my
  facets a bit, to go with the fancy prices —
Maybe it could be done under will? —
But I couldn't think that overnight I could transform inept
  vacant housewife Elsie into Saint Sophia the Gnostic Gnoddess
  of Holy Wisdom —
Maybe not into Saint Sophia, but what about Sophie – Sophie
  Firebright!? —
And the Squire? Perhaps Squire Pigspurt! *Spanking Squire
  Pigspurt*!! —
There was a knock at the door and it was Buster's
  drummer —
Buster's drummer had become more obsessed with my nose
  than I was —
he'd knocked up a little place for my nose lady, —

cut away edge of box

a box set (in fact made of an apple box) —
a miniature boudoir —
with dressing table and mirror —
and with my nose stuck in —
(and this I suggest was the achievement) —
it was more sexy than funny.

Pigspurt! 'twould be true to say that there was now a most
   decided nasal excitation to life! —
Sometimes I feared 'twas something worse: Nasal Infestation! —
That somewhere along the line, I had allowed into my nose
   some sort of daemonic urge —
That the daemon Pigspurt had taken up residence in my nose, —
and I was now to be led places, literally, by the nose —
Certainly it was something way beyond Stuart Pearce impressions
   that I was into now —
Sometimes blasphemous poetry would ring in the thing, like:

> *'Here come the Noz, the Noz of Nozareth*
> *Also known as the Nozarene.*
> *I say to one "Go!" and she goeth,*
> *I say to another "Come!" and she cometh.*
> *I say to another "Do this!" and she dothitheth it.'*

(It's only right to warn you, that we've now reached the point in
the proceedings which Claire Armitstead of the *Guardian* found
'bemusingly unfunny'.)

THE ADVENTURES OF PIGSPURT

A map of London, and the pins stuck in it mark the points
   of my major nasal adventures across the capital —
Of course, I would argue it to myself in this way: that it
   was research —
That I was researching what would undoubtedly become a
   British classic erotic nasal novel —
Where is such a thing? —
The French threw down the gauntlet with *Cyrano de Bergerac
   (Version Bleu)* —
The Italians replied with *Pornochio* —
Ours will be: *The Adventures of Pigspurt* —
And what, pray, will we find in those pages? —
Well, let's just have a look at some of the research, shall we? —
Location 14: Finsbury Park – the actual park —

I had on my flying helmet, my usual headgear for a night
   on the snout —
There's a not unpleasant café in Finsbury Park – certainly
   the coffee's drinkable —
and in there I got into pleasant chat with a woman in her
   mid-thirties —
À propos of not a lot, I said: 'Have a look at my nose —
Does it make you think of anything?' —
Well no, it just looked like a nose to her —
So I pointed out the secret of it: the cleavage and the thighs
   and wotnot —
She was amused by the concept —
So I went out to the car and I brought in the Boudoir Box —
She went hysterical —
And then I told her about my scheme —
that I was combing the land for her whose arse matched my
   nose —
And she was up for it! —
Wheeeeeeeeeeeeeee! —
And we were round the back of the toilets —
with the Polaroid! —
Well, one thing led to another —
And in the middle of the another, I thought:
I know the name for this —
this is cunninasus! —
Coitus Proboscidalis!! —
And then with her legs akimbo, like the flesh wings of an
   aircraft, and me in my Biggles hat —
Fundamental orifice, my intercom! —
And I suddenly started broadcasting more of my poem up it:

'Here comes the Schnozz,
the Schnozz of Schnozzareth,
Also known as the Schnozzarene . . .'

And then I was subject to a roaring of form, —
proboscidoidal extension! —
then (actual or illusory, I know not) ejaculation! —
Not that I snotted up her —
more that a pinnacle blowhole had been miraculously and
    momentarily formed for the occasion —
As I pulled out, I thought: I hope I haven't made her preg-
    nant —
and she'll give birth to a bogey baby —
I looked up and there was the Park Keeper —
'How's Alf?' he said.

Location 7 is of interest I think. Location 7 was a Malay
    lady who ended all her sentences with 'innit' – ('n' it?) —
What I mean is, invariably and ludicrously, —
e.g: 'I like your hat, do you want a cup of tea, innit?' —
Sometimes she'd mint Zen koans: 'Can you pass the sugar,
    innit?' —
Something amazing could occasion the further addition of 'nell'
    – [Nell: poss. abbr. 'Fucking Hell'] —
as: '. . . she snorted it *all* up and got completely out of it,
    innit, nell!' —
    And so I called her 'Innit Nell' —
Anyway, regarding this cunninasus stunt, she declared herself
    to be 'Really inuit, innit' —
Really Inuit! —
I said, 'So you're really Inuit Nell? —
You're Inuit Nell! Eskimo Nell!!' —
She didn't get it – ('I don't get it, innit,' she said) —
But she wanted me to go along to this club she knew —
She thought that some of the members of the club might
    be 'inuit' too —
She warned me that there was a strict dress code at the club —

I said, 'Well you can count me out if you like. I don't like
     going to places where they force you into a dickie-bow tie
     and all that' —
But that wasn't her meaning, no no. 'Just put your Biggles
     hat on, innit!' —
Anyway, this club is just off the Charing Cross Road, round
     the back of Foyles, and it only meets on a Monday —
and it's called the Scented Crowbar —
They let me in, but once inside I felt overdressed in my flying
     helmet —
The first guys who riveted one's gaze were old fat men —
One of them looked like my old Latin master —
And all they'd got on . . . —
what they must have done is, they must have each removed
     the cylindrical core from a toilet roll, then wrapped them
     round with gaffer tape, and then stuck their plonkers in –
     tied them up round the back, and shoved a few daffodils up
     their bums —
There were fifty-year-old cubs there, with a sort of Mrs Denn
     cub-mistress type, ready to slipper them round the back of
     the legs if they got out of order —
And then there were bishops there —
and Venuses in Furs —
But in the main the ladies of the Scented Crowbar adopt
     this mode: leotards cut high, and fishnet stockings, very
     high-heeled shoes, bunched up Charlie Chesters, and a little
     'floggaroo' tucked under the arm —
This berky chap in studded codpiece comes up and says: 'How's
     Alf?' —
I tell him he's all right —
'Oh look!' says my new chum who did film reviewing for
     Time Out, 'See him over there?' —
Him over there is what had looked to be mini-skirted starlet —
'See him? He's the Head of the Art Department of the Romford
     Comprehensive —
And he's married to that fat dominatrix over there —

We didn't half have some fun over their place last week —
We'd got the block and tackle out, and we'd hoisted Ted
   up to the ceiling, —
(Where's Ted? – You'll meet Ted!) —
and he was all gagged and bound, just his arse hanging out
   waiting for his wallops —
And then somebody there actually knew what the Footsie 100
   Index is, and we got so interested in that, that we forgot about
   Ted!' —
The bar prices in there were really quite reasonable —
And there was disco music playing —
You'd get toilet-roll beplonkered old Latin masters dancing
   with bishops, and on one occasion some fellow who'd come
   as Frank Bough —
And I thought, What harm in it? It's just people who like
   to dress up . . . —
But then the music changed —
The disco music's gone, and now there's unhealthy church
   music playing —
of an order to separate the Bishops from the boys —
And onto the stage was trolleyed a mighty set of mediaeval
   stocks —
And the first up onto the stage was the Head of the Art
   Department of the Romford Comprehensive —
He offers his hands and head to the stocks —
And he's padlocked in by a beefy dominatrix lady —
Now joined by a partner —
they yank down his fatuous knicks —
and it's going to be canes first. —
If you went to a school where they practised corporal punishment,
   when someone's getting it, you always do one thing:
You count! —
Whack! goes the first lady, Whack! the second: Two —
Three! ... Four! ... Five! ..... Eight! .... Eighteen! ....
   Twenty-five!
Phorr! —

And then fresh ladies are called for —
High cut leotards and little 'floggaroos'! —
the cat-o-nineteen tails —
And they whisk him with the cat-o-nineteen tails for another
    twenty-five —
And again fresh ladies called for! —
I don't know where they get these things from: like over-sized
    table tennis bats (I guess you apply to a short-sighted ping-
    pong club) —
Anyway, when you've got one of these things, you screw wicked
    studs in it —
And he gets another twenty-five with the studded ping-pong
    bat —
Then he's let out, and up comes a toilet-roll beplonkered Latin
    master to get his regulation seventy-five! —
I count five of them through the stocks and by that time,
    I thought, God I've got to have a piss! —
The thing is, I'd put off going to the Gents in this place —
I thought it might be a bit chummy for my taste —
But I've got to go now! —
And it was like a torture chamber in there! —
There were guys had been craned right up to the ceiling,
    all gagged and chained —
There's this bloke up on the ceiling, all zipped up in a backwards
    helmet —
and he says: 'If you just want to have a pee, go in the Ladies' —
There's a real beefy pair of ladies in the Ladies —
Fishnet stockings? —
They'd be happier in sprout bags —
Anyway, they were fixing up thumb screws and horse whips for
    later in the evening, and I thought, I'm not getting it out in
    here! —
And the main event in the ballroom now was a free-for-all —
About nineteen old gentlemen's arses – bared and thrust into
    the podium – and nine or ten of these fine ladies walloping,
    and lashing round them with whips and bats —

And I thought, They must have filthy Gods these guys! —
And then they looked like so many sick old noses to me,
    these arses —
A nasal nightmare! —
And suddenly I thought NO – I'VE GOTTA GET OUT! —
And I had a piss in the side doorway of Foyles.

Now this was the odd thing: coming up Charing Cross Road —
(and usually I can tell the difference between a hallucination
    and a thing, and this was definitely a thing) —
was a NOSE —
or rather somebody in a nose outfit —
You could see his little feet coming through the nostrils of
    his nose costume —
I thought, Wow! What club's he been to?

When I got home from the Scented Crowbar, the front door
    was swinging wide open and there was no one in —
I'd been burgled —
They'd taken the television set, they'd taken the video
    recorder —
they left me the remote —
(and a whoopsie on the carpet) —
and they'd taken the word processor (sort of good news that) —
BUT they'd taken a load of my papers – including the *Pigspurt
    Diaries*.

In Homerton Police Station, the duty officer, when there was
no one around, said: 'If you take my advice Mr Campbell,
you'll leave the area, otherwise you'll wind up dead one night
– or worse. Not everyone here is your friend' —
And he concluded by shuffling his papers – (a bit of biz he'd
learnt off ITN) —
When I got back home it seemed to me that I owned too
much stuff —
I got the bin bags out, and I thought: I don't need this any
more, I don't need these, and I don't want anyone finding
that! —
And then through the 'postofis letahol' came a leaflet —
from the Victims of Burglary Support Group —

Dear Victim of Burglary,
You are probably doing one or other of these things now: . . .

And one of them was: stuffing all your gear in bin bags
to chuck out —
And then a phone call from the Victims of Burglary Support
Group —
Would I like one of them to come and chat with me? —
Have a sit with me? —
Well . . . No. NO! —
I was beginning to put two and two together in a rather sinister
way —
I thought the odds were that it was the cops —
It was the cops, obviously, who'd come in and thieved all
my gear! —
And the Victims of Burglary Support Group? —
They're just part of the evil machinery —
They just want to grind you down, and squeeze a bit more
information out of you —
So I said: 'No no, don't worry about me. I'm fine thank
you' —
But I carried on throwing my stuff out —

But then the bin men, instead of properly slinging my stuff
   in the back of the cart —
They took my stuff in with them —
Into the driver's cab . . . —
(Incidentally, I found that with the TV remote I could make
   the neighbour's cat run up the curtains) —
Anyway, I wrote a stern letter to whoever was now in charge
   of investigating my garbage:

Dear Sir/Madam,
Why don't you just come out into the open!? Tell me what
you want instead of this rather childish James Bond
routine.

And I posted the letter into my dustbin.

I tell you one thing, I'd hung up my spurting helmet for good
   and all now —
And any time I was away from home, I'd take the opportunity
   to write myself a letter —
in disguised handwriting, on a borrowed typewriter, as if from
   a friend or a relative —
And they'd heard about the nonsense I'd got into —
Listen, we all know this don't we: All men of a certain age
   . . . they get into some nonsense or other —
And they'd all heard about my recent silliness and they were
   just *so pleased* that I'd got through it without any need for
   psychiatric help . . . —
It was just so I could receive these things – and screw them
   up and put them in my bin —
To settle things —
But then Buster Bloodvessel and the whole buggering band
   burst in —

Buster had now written the Song of my Nose —
'**** Nose!' —
And he was going to be launching it that night in the George
    Robey pub in Finsbury Park —
There was no oddsing it: I was picked up bodily by the band
    and carried out in some sort of triumph to the blue Transit
    and off to the George Robey —
Amazing gig – but then comes the moment I'd been dreading —
and the spotlight fingers the hall and finds me – and Buster
    points my nose out to the world!
Its thighs, its pubes and how it's inspired this next song:

But while they were playing I saw it! —
If such a thing does exist I saw it! —
The womanly posterior which matches my nose! —
Yes, yes, my darling, mmm, YARCHH!! —
Arghhh! —

Oh no! My nose in three and blood everywhere —
The fiancé of the phenomenon had read my mind —
And I was carted out and off to Homerton Hospital.

The specialist in Homerton said, 'Well it's a mess. You're
going to need rhinoplasty' —
Rhinoplasty? Apparently a word simply meaning to fix up your
nose —
'But,' he said, 'You can have it done like anything you like
now' —
And when he said that, there was this chunky little nurse
called Tracy who was filling in some sort of medical thing,
bending down, and indicating her chummy buttocks, I said,
'Can I have it done like that?' —
And she was really quite tickled by that, Tracy was —
and we became quite good friends —
(just friends – there was nothing nasal about this) —
When they let me out of the hospital, Tracy said that her
mother wanted to meet me —
Listen, I think if you've got a mother like Tracy's you should
give a bit more warning than she gave —
Tracy's really quite short, but her mother Olive is really quite
tall —
Olive embraced me warmly, kissed me on both cheeks and
said (this is our first meeting!): 'When you go to Australia,
go to Perth as well as Sydney, but you're thinking of going
to Canada first, aren't you dear? —
Why am I getting doughnuts?' —
She said: 'You've been very lazy about the Caribbean, haven't
you dear?' —
I said, 'Well I don't ever think about it' —
'What a shame,' she said. 'I can see you on the island of
Curacao, I can see you on Surinam, I can see you in Guyana —
When you go to Guyana ring this telephone number: Georgetown
72629 —

But you've got other islands in mind at the moment, haven't
   you dear? —
Six pigs from happiness – Is that a song? And what did
   happen to David?' —
I said, 'Look, what is this?' —
She said, 'Well, I don't know where I get anything from dear;
   why – was it any help to you?'

Anyway, I rather got into Tracy's mum Olive —
Olive loved a tipple —
(Tipple! Some nights we *swam* together) —
Olive took a great deal of interest in the figurines —
It was Olive's opinion that the figurines represented an attempt
   at communication by the late Captain Charlie Charrington —
She said, 'The first one you found was which dear?' —
'The Dog-dragon,' I told her —
'And what was the first thing you thought of?' —
'I saw the face of Captain Charlie Charrington' —
She said, 'Well there you are dear, that's the Captain saying:
   "Dear Kenneth, this is your Captain speaking" —
And then you found the Legs —
Is there anything wrong with your legs, dear?' —
'Well, I have to click my hip every now and then' —
She said, 'Well maybe you should be clicking it more, dear
   – I don't know —
But,' she said, 'it's really clear what the Captain's saying with
   the Shrieking Monk —
What he's saying is: "I have things of theological importance
   for you, but I am gagged."
You must seek to remove the Captain's gag, dear —
and you'll do that by way of your legs, no doubt —
Maybe you've got to go on a hiking holiday, I don't know —
Or maybe you've got to "consider legness" —

Drape your legs, perhaps? *Who's Sophie?'* —
'Where did you get Sophie from?'
'From your map dear!' —
She took a ball of knitting wool out of her bag —
(in trance, she smirks, Olive) —
and with the wool she joined up my nasal adventure flags
   in such a way that they spelled out:

THE ADVENTURES OF PIGSPURT

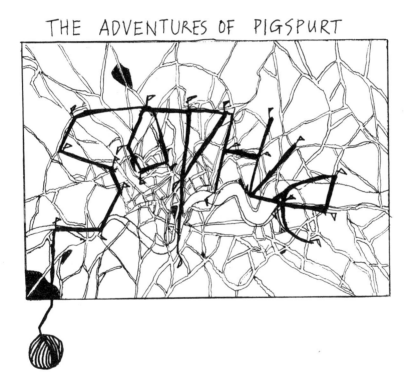

I found myself making a full confession of everything to Olive —
Olive said, 'I think it's all very clear, isn't it dear? —

Everything is telling you that it's time now to soft-pedal on this
rather alarming side of your personality, the Squire Pigspurt
side, your Spanker, and time now to be stressing your softer,
your Sophie side' —
And Olive had the goodness now whenever she came round
to see me, always to sit to the right of me – to draw out
my Sophieness —
And then one evening, she said:
'A shop has just come in dear; it's round the back of Euston
station; it's in a road that begins with E; and it's next door
to the bookies, this shop; —
you'll think it's a television repair shop —
Go in there, dear —
There's a lady in there and she's something of a healer and
she may be able to help you, dear —
Tell her that you're having spiritual counselling.'

Well, I think the road referred to is Eversholt Street —
And next-door to the bookmakers is not a television repair
shop —
But there's a sign in the window saying: TV Wear —
You can't see in through the windows, they're black – opaque —
the name of this shop is Transformation —
I can't speak too highly of the staff of Transformation —
The ladies who serve and advise are real ladies —
(I'm sure they are . . . yes, they are) —
They pointed me towards the free coffee —
Free coffee in Transformation —
And I browsed around their wares —
Eventually finding myself in easy conversation with a lady whose
name tag informed us she was S. Heila ('Healer?') —
I said, 'I don't know what I'm doing here at all, actually —
I'm having spiritual counselling, and it is true that I'm meant

to be bringing out my feminine side a bit more, but I hadn't
thought I was meant to go tarting around the town!' —
S. Heila said: 'No no, you're having spiritual counselling. I
understand —
Has there been a name given to your female side yet?' —
I said, 'Yes, well there has, I suppose, yes: Sophie. Sophie
Firebright' —
'So,' she said, 'Sophie would be like an older woman who's
had all her babies?' —
'Yes,' I said, 'I suppose she would.' —
'She sounds to me, your Sophie, as if she's an environmental
lady —
Have a look at this – this is an environmental top' —
(handing me a cream blouse with built on green scarf) —
'What makes it environmental?' —
'I don't know really,' she said, 'but Greenpeace came in and
bought six.' —
She showed me a black skirt which apparently went very nicely
with the environmental tops —
And then she put a wig on me —
'to help me towards my Sophie' —
I said, 'S. Heila? What does the S stand for?' —
'Sheila,' she said —
'Sheila Heila?!' —
'No no no,' she said. 'There was a glitch in the machine when
it stamped it out —
It should just say "Sheila"' —
She said, 'So you're not going to be wearing any of this stuff
out and about then?' —
'No,' I said, 'absolutely not! I can only suppose that perhaps
I'm meant to sit about in it during my spiritual counselling
sessions' —
'In that case,' she said, 'I should be thinking about buying
a set of these —
If the object of the exercise is to make a visual impression on
other people, well, you can put what you like in your bra —

But if it's for *you* – these are the answer —
These are really quite weightier than you'd suppose, hold them,
    go on —' —
They were a mixture of medical and naughty —
Surprisingly weighty —
and CHEEKY! with a life of their own —
I would compare the experience with that of handling
    ferrets —
I went slightly hysterical in the grip muscles —
'You glue them to your chest, and you actually will get the
    feel – the swing and wotnot, of real bosoms.' —
But this stuff isn't cheap —
The environmental top is £39.99, —
£29.99 for the skirt that goes nicely with it, —
£59.99 for the wig; bra £19.99; shoes £49.99 —
But silicon bosoms range from £99 a pair to £350! —
And there was no point in me thinking I could get away
    with £99 ones either —
A fellow of my build would get hardly any benefit at all —
No swing or wotnot from those —
I'd have to start thinking from £175, and it's not going to
    stop there because then I'm going to need the Dow Corning
    Medical Adhesive at £29.99 a pot to stick them on —
and Dow Corning Medical Adhesive Remover at £24.95 a bottle
    to get them off —
And then you need the blue stuff to rub in after you've had
    all this stuff on —
This is insanity, I thought. I haven't got that sort of money
    anyway!

But what's a Barclaycard for?

When I got it home, I hid it until Olive came round —
And I said, 'Olive! – "television repair shop"!' —
She was quite amused, and said: 'Come along then dear, let's
    see you in your Sophies' —
'There's a revolution due in ladies' blouse buttons, isn't there?'
    I said to Olive, donning the gear —
'That's not really a button, and neither's that really a buttonhole!
    Fffiddle fiddle fiddle!' —
'That's the whole point dear,' said Olive. 'That's the spiritual
    worth of this exercise: to calm you down' —
And it was true, only with a genuine inner serenity could
    I cope with my blouse buttons —
Anyway I got it all on me, and it was quite amusing for
    a minute or two —
And then – and I really don't know how this happened, but
    there we were having ever such a nice chat like us ladies
    who've had all our babies do have —
And this became the form of things – when Olive popped
    round, if I was alone and not expecting company, she'd say:
    'Just slip into your Sophies, dear' —
I recall such very pleasant tender times —
But then she wanted me to go further —
To go out in my Sophies —
I said, 'No no no no no! There's absolutely no point in going
    out in it —
It's just pleasant what we do, I love it like this —' —
But one Wednesday evening she said: 'Come on dear, let's
    just go along to the Spiritualist Church —
It's healing night tonight; not many people go; nobody will
    pay you any attention in any case —
Where's your spirit of adventure, Sophie?' —
The Spiritualist Church is only half a mile away —

but that's quite far enough in high heels —
Stamford Hill —
I'm talking about that one with the big spire —
  and that winged cow on it —
Just a small congregation, —
no more than fifteen people —
But they'd gone to a lot of trouble with the candles business —
candles all over the place, and a fellow there playing the organ
  with warts —
I sat towards the back —
In the congregation was this elderly Caribbean lady, her shoulders
  hunched with age —
But it was her white beret which singled her out for my atten-
  tion —
I always spot out people wearing berets, and that's because
  of my mate of some years ago, Chris Langham —
Langham was always obsessed with the notion that he'd never
  do anything so wonderful that his name would live forever —
He reckoned if you wanted your name to live forever, you'd
  got to find some common or garden object which hadn't been
  named yet, and then give it your name —
Just before Christmas one year, he summoned everyone he
  knew to this hall —
Eventually he came out in front of us wearing only a little
  black beret —
And he pointed to the little whisp thing on the top, and said: —
'Ladies and Gentlemen: a langham!' —
We all helped Christopher out that year —
We bought everyone we knew berets for Christmas, so we
  could go into Harrods (etc.) demanding: 'A beret please.
  With a particularly chunky langham!' —
And that's what the elderly Caribbean lady had —
(her name was Ethel incidentally) —
a beret with a particularly chunky langham.

Of course it became a little bit regular, this popping along
   on a Wednesday to the healing with Olive —
On the fifth occasion, actually sixth, no fifth – Ethel wasn't
   there —
And when we came out, Olive said: 'I think we should go
   and call on Ethel dear.' —
I said, 'Well you can count me out, I'm going home!' —
'Come along dear, she's a very infirm and elderly lady; now
   come along' —
Ethel lived in those flats for old women round the back of
   Safeways and she was in bed in her beret —
Her old legs didn't work any more —
And Olive said: 'You know Sophie don't you? Sophie
   Firebright?' —
And then she said: '*Sophie does healing*' —
I went hot then cold and then had the feeling I was not
   the owner of my body —
(that I'd been renting it, maybe) —
And this is what I heard bursting from my lips:
'*Mi bagaff hasmali, Ma bagaff himani, Ani lo yudiah haloutz
   ma kazi* —
Who's on the left-wing, What's on the right-wing, I Don't
   Know is centre forward, Ethel —
*Im fulugud dei. Im fulugud dei blong yumitufala pushem lilfala
   salwata wanae —*
insaed postofis letahol blong praefala pasta —
talim – 'ski aelan twinki twink plantifala ia!' ' —
And she was looking up at me – impressed, trusting —
And in demi-trance, I picked up the scissors and snipped off
   her langham —
And I passed her hatpin through the chunk of the langham
   making a simple crucifix which I pinned on her —

And I said, 'No pies —
No pies, there's no pies for you, Ethel – there's going to
  be NO PIES for you when you get Up There.'
And I kept repeating, 'No pies . . . No pies,' until I had
  tears streaming down my face —
'No pies, no pies. No pies, Ethel, unless you get up and
  give us a little walk around the room' —
And I was massaging her old legs now '. . . no pies . . .' —
and so was Olive '. . . no pies . . .' —
Olive was now singing her all-purpose interdenominational
  hymn —
'No pies, tra-la-la' —
And we got Ethel up, and we gave her a little trot round
  the room —
And we laid her back to bed and I said: 'Ani rotzah lekuleff
  tapuzeem!' —
'We ladies must peel oranges.' —
When we got out, Olive was hysterical —
She said; 'I think you've got the gift dear!' —
And when we got back, we polished off a whole bottle of
  Jamesons —
Olive went flakey on the sofa and had to stay the night —
The next week, Olive wasn't around —
Sometimes she had Spiritualist duties in Stoke-on-Trent or
  Iceland —
I think it was Stoke that week —
But it was Wednesday evening . . .
I thought: Well, I think I'm up to going to the healing
  on my own now —
So I put me Sophies on and popped off to the church.

And it was fine —
But Ethel wasn't there —

I thought, I know what Olive would like me to do; she'd
    like me to pop in on Ethel, make sure she's all right —
So I did; I popped in there, and Ethel was really much
    improved —
She was up and about —
She simply wasn't well enough to go to the healing —
She was reminiscing about her childhood in Guyana –
    GuyANNA, she called it —
And as she was remembering her girlhood chums —
I saw what a beautiful woman she'd once been —
And I rather felt an attack of the Pigspurts coming upon
    me —
She was fiddling around in the sink —
And I came up behind her, and I said: 'Ethel?'
She turned round – and I said:
'. . . Excuse me. There is something I must do!' —
And I got out of there —
Fled, like I was being pursued —
Cinderella at one minute to midnight! —
And as soon as I got in, I was throwing my gear off —
Bugger it! I thought. I've run out of blue stuff! —
And I was stuffing away my kit —
I thought, They're coming for me! —
They're coming for me tonight! —
But even so, there was to be a moment where I halted
    my disrobing —
I was dropping the skirt, when I stopped —
the skirt still draped halfway down my legs —
my legs look for all the world like the legs of the figurine! —
And in looking across to the Pair of Legs on the mantelpiece,
I catch sight of my own bare bum in the mirror —
UH HAHH! HA-HAHHH!! UH HA!!! HA! HAHHH!!!!
And I realized, *'t was my own arse I sought!* —
UH HAHH! HA-HAHHH!! UH HA!!! HA-HAHHH!!!!!
I thought, What's that noise? —
UH HAHH! UH-HAHHH!! UH HA!!! HA-HAHHH!!!!

And I realized: It's me. IT'S ME! I'm laughing like the
Bishop of Colchester! —
It's an ingenious way of laughing that actually, because there
comes a point when you can't remember what you were
laughing at —
You're just laughing because your last laugh was so *deranged*!
There comes a point though, where it dies down —
And you remember I mentioned before about my being subject
to attacks of paralysis?
'entropy of the bone marrow' —
It was setting in that night —
and there was a musty smell to the place —
And shuffling movements —
And I'd turn round but I couldn't see what was doing it —
Then I felt there to be a challenge in the air —
And I was fighting to put it into words —
And I was reaching into the unthinkable —
The unspeakable —
But maybe, if I attempted performance of the unperformable
I might **unscrew the inscrutable**! —
If I only dared —
If I could only persuade myself to —
GO UP MY OWN ARSEHOLE!

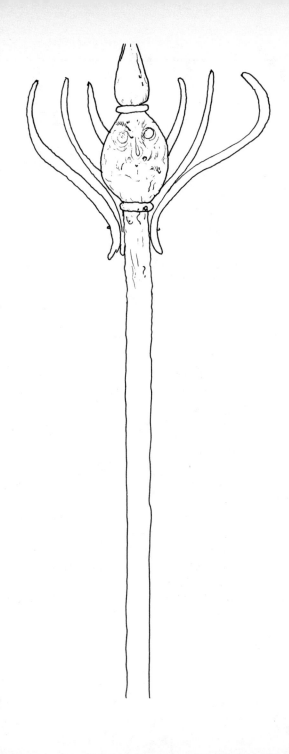

I could still see the room —
but hazily —
But then I was aware I was not alone! —
That I had a bearded visitor! —
'**In the most unlikely place, Kenneth**' He said —
'Just as Mrs Denn told you. In fact Mrs Denn and Miss
    O'Halloran hit the concept round about plumb centre' —
And He was going round the room, —
looking for clues! —
but with an *authority* —
I saw now how the business might be attempted without getting
    a laugh —
'Omniae viae ad Deum ducent!' He said; 'All paths lead
    to God. But some are quicker than others —
Your quick way was up your own arse *and you were born
    with the clue!*' —
I said, 'But I had my nose fixed; I had rhinoplasty —
I had it made to look like Tracy's . . .' —
'Yes yes,' He said. 'But we in our wisdom afflicted you with
    haemorrhoids! —
Walking that way, the tension and wotnot, soon got your
    bum back in nasal harmony! . . . —
Heaven and Hell, Kenneth, are basically the same place —
The good go to a good part of it, the bad go to a bad part of
    it, the fairly nice go to a fairly nice eternal picnic in a sort of
    park; louts lout around in the lout compound —
but *comedians sit with me*! —
Current favourites: Benny Hill, Eric Morecambe, and the Bishop
    of Colchester —

b'doom   b'doom   b'doom   b'doom

we have to keep sending the Grim Reaper down for cubs
    for him though! —
You see, they only think in these extreme forms of Heaven
    and Hell because of the absurdly enantiodromic nature of
    my set up here' —
I said: 'Wow, and that's it for all eternity then, is it, sir?' —
'That's it until I blow the whistle, dear boy,' He said —
'What happens then, sir?' —
'Well,' He said, 'I was thinking of blowing it quite shortly
    as a matter of fact —
Maybe next February or March —
After all, it's about time to get stuck in to some of that
    stuff that I let slip to Saint John the Divine —
Beasts with hundreds of eyes before and behind —
and the parting of the heavens, and the moving of the mountains,
    and the islands out of their places . . . —
But how tickled I am,' He said —
'How tickled I am that you found your way up to me so that
    we can have this farewell theophany before the Big Spring
    Clean —
You know, Kenneth, this hint of appalling pattern that you
    contrive to get in your stories? —
That is an intimation of the Divine —' —
'Wow,' I said. 'Is it really? But to do that I have to bend
    the truth a bit, you know —
Sometimes I put things out of their real order —
Sometimes I just invent things' —
'They are nonetheless intimations of the Divine!' He said —
'Yes,' I said, 'but don't I get my "God" a little bit grubby? –

and thus I'll get shunted to a less salubrious part of Heaven
– ? —' —
'Oh very much so!' said the Lord —
'But that doesn't sound quite fair to me then!' I said —
'So what is this Creation of yours then? A cock-up? A conspiracy?
    What is it?' —
'It is both!' said the Lord. 'Yours is an enantiodromic world —
But I disguised it —
But Heraclitus tumbled it —
So did Carl Gustav Jung and your Dick —
But all that was manageable —
But then, Kenneth, you started your Enantiodromic Two-Faced
    Acting Workshop Class Thingies —
Your Enantiodromic Two-Faced Acting Workshop Class
    Thingies are as much responsible for the need for a
    spring clean here as anything else —
If any of that stuff had got generally known, you would
    have unravelled the whole fabric —
The basic set-up here, humanitywise, is this:
The big guys get to whang between exciting extremes while
    the wankers hide in caves' —
I said, 'Am I to take it then, that your Commandments
    are to be seen as challenges?' —
'Oh very much so!' said the Lord. 'The Commandments!? —
The Commandments are only there to keep the berks in
    some sort of order! —
And out of the hair of the men of vision! —
    Churchill! . . . Maxwell! . . . the Mongol Hordes! . . . David
    DeNil! . . .' —
I was confused —
'I am hinge point,' He explained. 'Herman Melville wrote of
    me:

"Yea and nay, each hath his say,
But God,
He keeps to the middle way." —

I am balance and Satan is all around infinitely —
But I am infinity, and I try everything infinitely —' —
And the Lord had now picked up my Philip K. Dick Society
    Pamphlet:
'If you find this world bad, you should see some of the others,'
He read and nodded —
'Thus anything anywhere at any one moment is absurd —
The fragmentation being infinite —
But viewed *as a whole*, which is a perspective peculiarly mine,
    it is a pattern of full and infinite richness —' —
And the Lord had now picked up my *Ken Dodd: Laughter
    and Tears* by Gus Smith —
I said, 'We've met before, haven't we?'
'Mm hmm,' said the Lord —
'No, what I mean is, you've *appeared* to me before —' —
And I was racking through my thoughts . . . —
I said, 'I know! It was you who barged into my dream and told
    me to tell David DeNil he'd got to go and see every live show
    that Ken Dodd gave for a year!' —
'Oh yes I love Doddy!' said the Lord. 'Live!' He qualified —
'I trust you approved of my intervention in his tax affairs?' —
'Oh yes certainly,' I said. —
'I thought I'd be sussed there!' said God —
'So,' I said. 'When Ken Dodd told David DeNil he was
    going to Efaté in the New Hebrides . . . —' —
'Oh that was me speaking through him!' said God —
'Wow, so Ken Dodd's pretty important in the current scheme
    of things then?' —
'Oh you always knew that!' said God, —
'Yes,' I said. 'But I tell you what I'm still foxed over: what's
    the link then between Ken Dodd and the Solomon Islands?' —
'Here's one!' said the Lord, turning to page 83 of the Gus
    Smith book . . .
'Ooh look!' said God. 'You've even underlined it.' —
(This is Doddy talking directly to Gus, and he's saying:)

*'I would definitely count myself as an expert on the subject of what turns a man on. After all, I'm a professor of tickleology. But let's take the sensual bits first. With a man, certain parts of a lady have definite appeal. Some are leg men, calf men, ankle or cheek men. **I'm an upper arm and shoulder man, that's definitely one of the nicest bits.***'

UH HAHH! HA-HAHHH!! UH HA!!! HA-HAHHH!!!!
'So Ken Dodd was a Solomon Islander in a previous life!' —
'Don't get into all that,' said God. 'Previous lives and wotnot! —
You're not equipped to deal with what's really going on!' —
'But something like that maybe,' I said —
God was now frigging about with my new VCR. 'Show
    me how this works!' He said —
'Actually' I said, 'I only know how to play a video on it' —
'Oh no!' He said. 'You can set these things up to record
    programmes up to a year ahead!' —
'Yes I know,' I said, 'but I've been busy. But I tell you
    what's worrying me,' I said —
'This beast with all the eyes before and behind and the mountains
    and islands moving out of their places Revelation business —
Is there anything any of us can do about that?' —
The Lord was poring over the Mitsubishi VCR instruction
    booklet —
'This manual is incomprehensible!' declared the Lord. 'In all
    the languages!' —
'Except Japanese,' I said.
'No it's complete garbage in Japanese!' – said God —
'Sorry – what? The parting of the heavens and the great
    pooof!? No, there's nothing that can be done about that,'
    He said, 'No! —
'Tis writ! —
Well,' He said. 'Look; I would hold it off *only* . . . if could
    be found a man of good heart who would undertake to go
    and see every live show Ken Dodd gives for a year' —

'Well,' I said, 'I'm afraid I don't believe in you any more sir —
I don't even *suppose* in you any more —
That really is too absurd —' —
'I AM INFINITELY ABSURD!' said the Lord —
His words slippered the backs of my legs and I subsided
    on my knees —
'Sir,' I said. 'sir! Will I ever be forgiven for my snouting,
    for my days of Pigspurting?' —
'*Your days of Pigspurting*?' said the Lord, cruelly impersonating
    my accent —
'What's your problem boy? You never intruded, did you? —
You were always invited up, weren't you?' He said —
'You charmed them with your Boudoir Box and wotnot! —
and there was nothing daemonic about that!' He said —
'He whom you thought of as Pigspurt, that was you! —
You allowed your own repressed self to manifest! —
You must face it Kenneth: you are a *funny* fucker! —
Recall if you will any of the reactions of your various partners
    to your cunnisneezus . . .?' —
'Well,' I said, 'hysteria, tittering' —
'Exactly so!' said the Lord. 'You was a Professor of
    Tickleology —
Did you know, the Solomon Islanders were into cunnisneezus
    from the dawning of mankind? —
Why do you think they wear those feathers in their noses? —
But if I may', He said, 'I'd like to hint this: when you
    got that old lady up and walking I WAS NOT THERE! —
What would you make of that statement, Kenneth?' —
I said, 'What, you mean there was merely angelic involvement?
    . . . Daemonic?' —
'THAT WAS PIGSPURT!' He said 'How's Alf?' —
And He disappeared miraculously through the wall.

I said. 'Oy! Come back! Get back in here! You weren't God!' —
'You summoned, Kenneth?' (Bearded Gent halfway through
   the wall) —
'Take off the beard!' I said —
. . . the beard came off easily —
He now stepped fully into the room —
And a curly-brimmed bowler appeared on his head —
'Captain!' I said —
'Thanks for looking after Dee,' he said —
'I just wrote to her a few times, and went to see her once,' I said.
'All it takes,' said the Captain —
'Now listen,' he said. 'That wasn't a theophany —
I was posing as God —
Celestial espionage – but even that's a cover —
I'm part of a bunch who are heretically attached to mankind
   and life as you know it —
We love you Life! But like an old dog —
And it's time now, to put Life out of its misery —
You don't want Johnny Div's Revelations here —
So we're going for a final ingression of novelty; implosion of
   the entire multi-dimensional continuum of space and time; the
   megamacrocosmos to go down the plughole as the hyperspatial
   vacuum fluctuations of paired particles (i.e., your universe)
   collides with its own ghost image after billions of years of
   separation —
Why do they all have these irrational feelings of loss? —
Because **nothing** is the natural state. **Something** is perversion:
In order to create chronological matter out of the Nothing
   Nowhere, the Great Perverter had to separate forwards from
   backwards, positive from negative, **matter from antimatter** —
And me and the crew think we can bring the two together
   and engineer an Apocatastasis —
Every subatomic particle (except photons) will cancel each
   other out, the entire Universe quietly disappearing up its
   own bumhole —
Merely the whimper that Tommy Eliot spoke of —

a little Wh-ha-hoo! —
and only photons will exist, and we will have liberated the
  Universe of Light from the Black Iron Prison of Matter! —
And all Life will find itself walking up the path of the Promised
  Garden —
This time (we trust) demanding full inclusion in the plans
  for Phase Two!'

'Phorr,' I said, then 'Wow! Look, I'm just talking off the top
  of my head at the moment, but this is how it sounds to me
  on this side of the veil:
I've got a little daughter – she's not so little any more, she's 14 —
  and I really looked after her —
not like you just seeing her four times in a lifetime! —
And I'd really like her to live on, mine. I want her to live on! —
I want her to live on and face it! Whatever it's going to be! —
The Revelations or what the fuck —
Without, actually, thank you, sir, your kindness of this Apocat-
  astasis' —
'Then book your tickets for Ken Dodd!' he said —
'The first messages will come through on the 13th of March
  1993 during the "What a beautiful day" sequence' —
I said, 'First or second house?' —
'Second – but only if you see the first' —
'Yeah,' I said. 'And then I'll wind up in the Solomon Islands!' —
'I expect so!' he said. 'Iconoclast of the Islands! A Conrad
  in reverse! Lord Ken!' —
He said: 'David's doing damn fine out there, —
Bigman Chief of Fuckwire Island and all that —
But time now draweth nigh for the Great Smasher of Icons —
  (those frozen moments of myth!) —
And I speak here of the ethics of cannibalism! —
Why do you think we sent back the soul of Richard Burton

to infest Anthony Hopkins? —
In order to give the guy the charisma to play Hannibal Lecter! —
And now you've had Jeffrey Dahmer! —
and some splendid tart's been at it! —
EATING PEOPLE IS BACK! —
Bone up on your Dodd! —
We'll tell you when we're ready for you in the cradle of
   cannibalism —
David's already conquered the Northern islands, you'll move
   in at the South —
You'll meet up round about Fukkabukka —' —
I said: 'What and then I'll have to eat David?' —
'See how it goes!' he said, and he came forward, and he
   gripped me lovingly by the upper arm:
'There'll be pies,' he said —
'Excuse me —
There is something I must do —' —
And the whole theophany —
(or Captophany as it turned out to be) —
had lasted a mere nanosecond . . .

The Solomon Islanders embraced Christianity under the impression that they would thereby receive the wealth and possessions of the White Man. When this did not happen for them, they supposed they'd been tricked. That they'd been given cut or censored Bibles with the magic missing. It's now reliably reported that on the islands of Malakula, Erromango, and Tafea, that the gags and routines of Kenneth Dodd* are regarded as the lost gospels. And if on the 13th of March I'm called to join that priesthood 'tis with a sense of honour I shall chomp upon the Host.

*That's where I whisk off the wartyfala mask revealing the Melanesian Devotional Doddy, sometimes to an audible gasp.